Learning to Shoot

John Humphreys
Learning to Shoot

With photographs by DAVE PARFITT

ANDRE DEUTSCH

By the same author

Living off the Land
Hides, Calls and Decoys
The Sportsman Head to Toe
Modern Pigeon Shooting
Stanley Duncan, Wildfowler
The Do-It-Yourself Gameshoot
The Shooting Handbook '82–3
The Shooting Handbook '83–4
The Shooting Handbook '84–5

First published 1985 by
André Deutsch Limited
105 Great Russell Street London WC1

ISBN 0 233 97762 7

Filmset in Times Roman 10/12pt
by Falcon Graphic Art Ltd
Wallington, Surrey
Printed in Great Britain by
Ebenezer Baylis and Son Ltd, Worcester

For David and Peter

The ultimate ambition of every shooting boy – out alone with his own gun.

Contents

Introduction

The late Tim Sedgwick was a former distinguished editor of *Shooting Times*, a man whose evocative, knowledgeable, weekly column written under his pen name, 'Tower Bird', inspired and initiated a whole generation of shooting folk. Of his books, one of the best was *The Young Shot*, published in 1940, which gave a thumbnail sketch of the shooting scene of the day, was full of sound advice for youngsters entering the sport and contained plenty of hard facts. These, if the reader absorbed them carefully, would see him safely through the early steps of a shooting career.

Times have changed and the last thirty years have seen unsuspected pressures, new legislation, shifting public opinion and revised practice by shooting men. The emergence of the over and under shotgun, the reduction of the list of shootable species, the decline of the annual rook shoot, the boom in clay busting, new equipment made of exciting new materials – these and other changes, some more welcome than others, have taken place since *The Young Shot* first appeared on the bookshelves.

Thus, the newcomer to our sport at this, the end of the twentieth century, must consider new things and has a responsibility to be fully alive to the implications of conducting what may be felt by many in this modern era to be a difficult sport to defend. No one book could cover the whole field in depth, but *Learning to Shoot* is to be a companion for the teenager or possibly the more mature entrant to what is still an exciting, demanding and wholly worthwhile sport. The book will show him the codes, practices, skills, quarry species, etiquette, dogwork, hard and software of which he ought to be aware before setting forth.

Once he has read and assimilated the contents, the rest is up to him.

John Humphreys
Bottisham 1985

Boys in the beating line help flush a cock pheasant.

1
Shooting Today

When I was ten years old, an aged, bewhiskered farmer asked me, quite out of the blue, if I would like to shoot a rabbit. He knew I was already interested in such things, had an air rifle and already kept my ferrets well supplied with sparrows. He handed me a 12-bore shotgun and two cartridges, little knowing that never in my short life had I fired such a monster and barely knew how to operate the thing. I held my peace and admitted nothing as I, a small figure inwardly quaking, and he, striding out in his gleaming brown leather gaiters, walked over the stubble. My earnest prayer was that no rabbit would appear, least of all in a place where I would be expected to shoot it. It was not to be, for we had walked barely a score of paces when, with a dry rustle and puff of dust, a rabbit exploded from beneath a wisp of straw at our feet and set off like a good-'un for the hedge, fifty yards away.

It was clearly my shot, but I stood rooted to the spot, as mesmerized as the rabbit itself would have been when confronted by a stoat. In that highly charged few seconds the world seemed to stand still, but Mr Tarry, in one smooth, easy movement, allowed the gun to float to his shoulder, touched it lightly and, bang! Just as it seemed safety was at hand the rabbit rolled over and over in a series of somersaults, a blur of white and hodden-grey, and lay still. I ran to fetch it, all warm, floppy and quite dead. 'Sorry,' grunted Mr Tarry, 'couldn't wait.'

It was a small enough incident in itself, and he need not have apologized for saving me from certain disgrace; far from it, for in that magic moment when his gun had flown so easily to his shoulder and the bolting bunny had rolled over with a certain clinical finality, he had given me an insight into a new world and sparked off an ambition to be able to do what he had done, even if it meant devoting my whole life to it. Let all the other boys, if they wished, go off and become engine drivers; I was going to be a shooter and master the thrilling skill which I had seen demonstrated.

However, it was a full year before I was to fire a shotgun in anger or even have one in my hands. Father being a country parson, it was not surprising that I found myself from time to time in the company of the sexton. The churchyard lay beyond the rank of elms and limes and the rambling shrubbery of the vicarage garden. The sexton possessed a battered old 12-bore which he kept with his spades and other equipment – indeed, he referred to it as a 'tool'. It was his custom, as he was digging away, to keep an eye on the elms, and when a pigeon landed on a bare bough or began cooing loudly from the shadows of the bee-buzzing limes, that aged, angular man became a coiled snake, a stalking panther. Clutching the gun menacingly, making use of every gravestone and scrap of cover to conceal his approach, he worked his way within range. He took careful aim; there was an ear-splitting bang, and the pigeon tumbled down into the nettles whence I, my short trousers baring my knobbly knees, retrieved it. The sexton did not hold with flying shots – too risky and wasteful of ammunition – he was only after the vital ingredient of a pigeon pie which, in those hard times, was quite a feast.

At first I was forbidden to lay a finger on the gun; he told me that if I did so, he would (by some hidden powers) know it instantly and I respected the rule. But eventually I was allowed to do the shooting, was issued with two red cartridges and strict instructions not to miss, and sent off into the bushes where I lurked in wait for the next unfortunate pigeon to arrive. With hindsight I realized that this crazy old fowling piece was a death trap – a thing to give a gunsmith or safety officer nightmares for a month. Only one hammer cocked, the other falling loosely back and forth. The action was so loose that the brass cartridge head detached from the cardboard each time you fired. It should, by rights, have been condemned years before. For all its faults, even the one that it might have blown my head off at any moment, it was my first experience with a shotgun and so has become a treasured and hallowed memory.

Such was the shaky start to a shooting career which has spanned about thirty-five years. It might still be possible for a youngster to start in such a way today, but is less easy than it was then. Today we are more aware of matters of safety: most (but not all) of the rattletrap 'farm guns' have gone to their last home. General knowledge about guns and shooting is vastly improved, while the clay coaching ground, British Association for Shooting and Conservation courses and teach-ins in addition to a wealth of up-to-date literature and advisory pamphlets make it less likely that the young shot will be left to his own devices to find out as he goes along.

There must still be room for an element of discovery in any
activity and shooting is no exception. What a pity it would be if we
found out everything second hand, if our good experiences were
orchestrated for us, if all our pleasures of finding out were dulled
by officious adults. Finding out for yourself is an important – I
would say vital – part of shooting, and adults who deny us that
pleasure do us no favour. Having said that, an adult must be on
hand to make sure that we comply with the law, do not put
ourselves or others at risk and shoot no protected species in places
where we have no authority to go. After that, a gentle guiding
hand, a hint here and there or the occasional provision of
transport, cartridges and opportunities are all we need from them.
The grounding in the basics, especially in matters of safety, is vital
and later on in this book we shall be looking at them carefully, but
parents and uncles must judge when they have given us enough
and when we can get on with all the fun of finding out.

As a would-be shooter you are joining an excellent, flourishing
and popular sport. It knows no class boundaries, for while the
more money and connections you have may mean better quality
sport and bigger bags, owning a shotgun is the right of every
British citizen (with few exceptions) and with a little energy,
initiative and care some sport can be found. Few farmers, for
example, would deny a keen shooter of proved safety and reliability permission to shoot his pigeons. Pigeon shooting will offer you
every type of shot in the book, and the bird is as testing as any that
flies – woodcock included. Shooting birds in the wood as they fly in
to roost will give you high, driven pheasant, while shooting over
decoys can produce springing teal, driven grouse, jinking snipe or
crossing partridge all on the same day. Pigeon shooting has been
termed a poor man's sport, and while that once may have been so,
the description does it scant justice today. There are those who do
nothing *but* pigeon shooting, claiming it to be the most testing
form of shotgun sport they know.

The pheasant is a common bird, and it is a poor farm without a
few on it somewhere. Rough shooting with the farmer's permission is also good fun; it is an adventure, where you are thrown on
your own resources and may depend on or blame no one but
yourself for the way things go. Ask the most hard-bitten and
experienced covert shooter and he is likely to say that the potter
round with dog, gun and maybe a good friend, are what he enjoys
as much as anything. To find such shooting you must beg
permission; maybe the farmer whose pigeons you shoot will
extend his invitation to 'have a walk round'. You must be prepared
for some rebuffs but persistence is usually rewarded in the end.

Alternatively, rough shooting, like most other forms of shooting, may be bought through one of the agencies or individuals advertising in *Shooting Times* and elsewhere. Buying shooting is not cheap and it must be carefully done for, as in most walks of life, there are some rogues around. Most reputable agencies or places personally recommended are usually safe enough and, as for the money, I have known boys who have worked in the harvest or at some other job to raise the cash, and others who have asked that their birthday and Christmas presents might come in the form of a day's shooting.

Wildfowling is another branch of the sport for which few resources are required. Your local pigeon club may be able to find you some pigeon shooting to get you started, and similarly, wildfowling clubs affiliated to the BASC will at least give you access to the foreshore and the chance at a duck or even a goose. Many clubs have junior sections, the Frodsham and District Wildfowlers Association in Cheshire being a case in point. There is a waiting list – you may have to resign yourself to that fact whatever club you join – but once you are in, there are meetings, good shooting and a programme of induction and education which are ideal for a newcomer to the sport.

Like the roughshooter, the wildfowler must learn patience and fieldcraft and, above all, resign himself to little or nothing in the bag. There will be times when the excitement and multitude of fowl will exceed his wildest dreams, but such experiences must be

Give a fast bird plenty of forward allowance.

earned. The fowler appreciates the genuine skills of shooting, of country wisdom, of concealment, marksmanship, bird identification and field craft. Most foreshores in England are controlled by the local club and they see to it that the marsh is not overshot and that their members conduct themselves with restraint and as true sportsmen.

However, it would be true to say that the shooting world is a good employer which has a thriving guns and accessories trade, deploys gamekeepers, supports research into game rearing and maintains spinneys, woods, cover-strips and the rich pattern of the English landscape. The driven shooter makes the largest cash input. This branch of the sport has evolved during the twentieth century, from Edwardian days when each great estate vied with its neighbour to see which could produce the record bag, to modern times when an appreciation of quality and sportsmanship has become a priority. Sadly, there are still estates which aim for huge bags, and still rich businessmen – many of them from overseas – who are prepared to pay the large prices which such days cost. To rear, keeper and show one pheasant on a driven day costs about £10.00, so such sport is beyond the range of most of us. In my opinion – and this is not sour grapes – this sort of shooting can quickly become tedious, especially when you realize that the same money would buy first-class wildfowling or rough shooting over a much longer period.

One in the bag: note the two ejected cartridge cases still in the air (left).

Most driven game shooting consists of a few farmer friends combining to drive their ground rather than strolling round rough shooting. In this way they have the chance at a driven bird which is in every way more challenging and exciting than one walked-up. A walked-up bird is, make no mistake, easy enough to miss, but a cock pheasant flying high and fast from the cover back to the home wood can be the most difficult shot in the book, and to bring one down is a matter of pride and delight. A driven shoot may produce ten birds or two hundred – to shoot more is overdoing it. To organize a drive you need a minimum of two people, one to beat and one to shoot. I have taken part in some thrilling two-man drives with a friend and his dog working a choked dyke, sprawling hedge or stream down to where I lurked at the end. As a refinement of the rough shoot, this is a tactic which ought not to be ignored.

More often, though, at least ten beaters and six standing guns are required to conduct a traditional driven day. There is, as we shall see, plenty of room on these occasions for boys and beginners, even if they are not necessarily armed. Grouse shooting is carried out on roughly the same principle as pheasant and partridge shooting: the birds may either be walked up or driven. Grouse tend to be expensive birds to shoot, because of their comparative rarity and because they cannot be reared and released. However, those who live in the high country, too bleak for pheasants, may just find that there is a sprinkling of grouse on the local mountain, too few to make organized shooting worthwhile but enough to give a keen and lucky lad a shot or two early in the season.

The local hare shoot is another opportunity for a young shot to see some sport. The grand hare shoot was once an annual event in many parishes, but declining numbers of hares have made them less common. Some still take place and there is always room for a keen, safe shot. Rabbiting is another traditional sport by means of which many old farmers developed a quick eye and an uncanny knack of snap-shooting. Myxomatosis put an end to that as a common sport, but there are still rabbits, more scattered, maybe, than in the old days and in nothing like the numbers, but they still live in holes; they still bolt when ferreted and then still give testing, quick shots for the safe and careful. All ground game is potentially hazardous from the safety point of view and especial care must be taken. We shall be looking at the vital matter of safety in a later chapter.

An aspect of shotgun shooting which may capture your interest and imagination is clay pigeon shooting. This is a spin-off or sub-group of field shooting which has a huge following with its own national association and network of local clubs. It calls for no field craft, dogwork nor knowledge of the countryside but has honed-in and concentrated purely on the skill of hitting a flying target with a shotgun. Nevertheless there are few branches of the sport that can give such pleasure. The clay 'bird' may be skilfully thrown to represent any animated target from a high pheasant to a bolting rabbit, from a jinking woodcock to a swooping crow. Its devotees enjoy trying their skill at a guaranteed number of targets – there is none of the lottery of a pigeon hide – and from your static position, there is no call to tramp boggy moorland or struggle through the brambles. Also, there may be some who do not feel happy, for a variety of reasons, at killing live targets but enjoy using a shotgun, so for them, clay shooting is the perfect sport.

Clay shooting may be enjoyed at many levels, from a group of amateurs with one trap on a quiet patch of farmland on a Sunday morning, to a highly competitive, almost professional level. The sport is an element in the Olympic Games and thus has an international standing. The tough competition is not to everyone's taste, so clays may be used to learn how to shoot, to sharpen your reflexes prior to the game season or a 'big' day, or you may pay your £1.00 and enter the shoot at your local country fair. For many, that is quite enough clays for a season, but a special few will catch the 'bug' and possibly go on to great things, to the exclusion of all their other hobbies.

So, the sport you are thinking of pursuing is alive and well, in good heart and full of challenge, variety and excitement. Few countries so crowded and industralized as Britain can boast such a wealth of wildlife or such a rich pattern of rural scenery. The reason for this is a long tradition of responsible farming practice and country sports which have ensured a proliferation and con- servation of desirable species and a control of crows, stoats, magpies, rats and feral cats which, if left to their own devices, would flourish at the expense of their less predatory neighbours. The woodlands planted by the sportsman for his foxes and pheasants will also harbour songbirds, badgers, wild flowers and butterflies in a whole series of mini-environments. Often they are a stark contrast to the surrounding, highly mechanized and intensely productive farmland. In the same way, the anglers clean the rivers, fight pollution, keep the river banks tidy and control predators. As a shooting man you have a responsibility to protect this heritage, to ensure that when your time comes, you pass on as much as, or more than was passed down to you. In the meantime, enjoy and make the most of the richness of your sport.

2
Apprenticeship

Many shooters start their careers with an air rifle. It used to be birdsnesting and egg collecting, but now that both are, very properly, outlawed, it is the air weapon which is our initiation into shooting. The first thing I ever shot was with a BSA Cadet air rifle borrowed from a friend. In a Scots pine tree on a naked branch sat a woodpigeon. It was a summer's evening of complete calm when the world seemed to stand still. I levelled the weapon, conscious of some horrific wobbles of the sights, and after an interminable wait, I pulled the trigger. With a fearful clattering of wings the bird tumbled down into the stinging nettles below whence, as I was to do a few years later with the sexton's gun, I retrieved it. From then on, I was hooked, but I did not appreciate the luck which had smiled on me, to allow me to hit a pigeon in the head with a .177 air rifle with open sights on an unfamiliar weapon. It was a rare combination of flukes, and many a pigeon did I fire at and miss thereafter.

A pigeon in a tree is a hard bird to stalk – air-rifle range is short and a pigeon is a sharp-eyed bird. I have shot many thousands of them since and my respect for their sense of self-preservation has increased rather than diminished. I did manage to bag a few with my air rifle, but it was only by the slowest and most careful stalking or by lying in wait for patient hours beneath a favourite roosting tree that I was able to come to terms with them. I was not aware of it at the time but I was learning the rudiments of field craft and a degree of self-sufficiency during these rather primitive man-oeuvres.

As for accuracy of shooting, the rarity of chances was the best incentive to ensure that shots were not wasted. It might take a week of waiting before a shootable pigeon presented itself, so the opportunity was not to be squandered. This taught care and accuracy and proved to me that practice, at first with tin cans, was necessary. My father had been persuaded to give me a rifle of my own and with this I found gradually that I could hit smaller and smaller targets, working down to an (old) penny and eventually even the heads of matchsticks. One learned to allow for the wind, for the drop of the pellet as the range increased and to apply the clinical precision required in all rifle shooting.

It is often said that good rifle shots are not good with the shotgun and vice versa. I can appreciate the theory and understand how a different set of skills and disciplines is required for each, but in my experience it is simply not so. I know numerous shooting men who are equally good with gun and rifle so, when you make a start with your airgun, do not allow yourself to be alarmed by those who may tell you that you are spoiling your chances as a shotgunner.

BSA no longer manufacture the Cadet or the Cadet Major of my boyhood, but they, Webley and other firms make an excellent range of air weapons to suit most pockets, and these are just right for lucky lads. Beware of spending too much money and buying too heavy a weapon for your size. To have to rely on finding a 'lean' for every shot can be very limiting. Being in the nature of an apprenticeship, the air-rifle stage is a short-lived period of your life, so it is not wise to spend a vast amount of money on one. It may be, as with clay shooting, that you decide to specialize in that branch of the sport; there are those who do and who take advantage of the range of super-weapons and telescopic sights available, enter competitions and become proficient at deadly accurate shooting at collared doves, crows, rats, grey squirrels, rabbits and other air-rifle quarry. Such shooters are in a minority, and most of us use the air weapon as a stepping-stone to shooting with the shotgun.

Before leaving the air weapon it is important to remember that even the most feeble of them is powerful enough to put out a human eye or commit some other ghastly injury. Each year there is a catalogue of accidents involving young people and air weapons; there are also those who, lacking proper guidance, shoot at cats, protected birds or damage property – so much so that there is a lobby demanding much tighter control of air weapons, and even some form of certification for their owners. Most safety is common sense and we will be examining the matter in depth in a later chapter. The greatest care must be exercised especially around buildings and near people. Remember that the pellet which misses or ricochets will fly on and strike – who knows where or what? The golden rule is always to shoot upwards or where some perfectly safe background, such as straw stack or a bank of soft earth, provides a backdrop.

The law on airguns is quite straightforward. If you are between

Vulcan de-luxe air rifle – a handy all-rounder.

fourteen and seventeen years of age you may not buy or hire an airgun but may borrow one or receive it as a gift from someone over seventeen. You may use the weapon on private property, where you have a right to be, without supervision. You may carry an unloaded air rifle (not an air pistol which is virtually useless for sporting purposes) in a public place only if it is in a securely fastened gun cover so that it cannot be fired.

If you are under fourteen years old the same restrictions apply, but you may not buy or hire an airgun or ammunition, and it is an offence for anyone to offer you one as a gift. You may use an airgun, but your parents must keep control of the weapon and supervise your use of it and also be with you when you carry it in public, as usual, in the securely fastened gun cover. Remember that should a pellet pass off your property and onto someone else's premises, both you and your supervisor have committed an offence. A public place means anywhere where the public are allowed to go, whether or not they have to pay. Roads, parks, footpaths and play areas are all examples of such places. It is also an offence to fire your airgun within 50 feet of the centre of a roadway or public footpath.

An airgunner tends to be eyed critically by the general public but if he is seen to be mindful of the interests of other country users, is dressed appropriately for his sport, goes only where he has permission and shoots no protected birds, not only will he be welcomed but also he will be sowing the seeds for future invitations in the days when he has graduated to the shotgun.

Legitimate quarry, including those I have already mentioned, will be feral pigeons, mice, all corvids, sparrows and starlings. The inedible part of your bag should, ideally, be used since no shooting man cares to bag anything which he cannot use in some way or which is not a recognized pest. Ferret owners are usually grateful for birds since feeding ferrets year in, year out can become a problem. Pigeons and rabbits should be eaten or given to those who will appreciate them. If you are shooting on a farm, it is courteous to offer your edible victims to the farmer – he will probably refuse, but you gain a good mark for doing the right thing.

As a spin-off from his lessons on marksmanship, field craft, camouflage and responsible, legal use of weapons, the budding air gunner will gradually absorb and learn to follow the Country Code. He will leave no litter; leave the ground as he found it with no broken bushes or gates left open; he will respect stock and crops and regard his use of the countryside as the privilege which it is. It is not such a formidable list of do's and dont's as it might at first seem, for most of it is common sense and common courtesy. An airgunner who has his share of both has two major attributes which will serve him well later on.

There are other ways of gaining access to the grown-up world of shooting. Shooting fathers, uncles, brothers or even family friends are usually keen to talk to you about their sport. It is a short step to being taken out with them on their expeditions. There is always room for a dog holder, game carrier and general dogsbody in the shooting field, and many a boy has learned in such a way. It is no good going unless you are observant and are eager to notice the finer points. When I was learning the ropes I spent many days in the field armed with no more than a walking stick. I found myself lugging hares which seemed almost as big as me, up endless fields of heavy ploughing, arriving at the far end more dead than alive,

There are plenty of things you can do to help on a shooting day.

plastered with clay and seriously wondering whether after all I had decided to enter the right sport. At other times they would send me to beat through what appeared to be impenetrable bramble patches or dense clumps of overgrown coppice with barely room for a rabbit to squeeze. I seemed never actually to flush any game and when I emerged scratched and exhausted at the other end, all the sport was over. All I had known of it was a series of distant shots as I was toiling in the brake.

More exciting was accompanying one or two men and their dog on a roughshooting or wildfowling expedition. So what if I had to carry the bag and struggle over ditches too wide for my little legs? I could share in the thrill of the chase, in watching dogs work a line of a running bird, jump to the explosive eruption of a pheasant from the dead reeds, hold my breath as it accelerated away, sure to escape. Then the shot would follow and the bird, one moment so strong, swift and purposeful, collapsed in a puff of feathers and fell to earth with a complete and exhilarating finality.

Organized beating on a properly run shoot is still a very good way to start. Usually you will be paid for your services and a good beater is worth every penny that he gets. Approach the local keeper and offer yourself as a beater; pressures of school may mean that you are limited to Saturdays and the winter holiday, but a keeper will welcome a loyal and regular addition to his team. Your job will be to take your place in a line of other beaters and walk through the cover wielding your stick and driving the birds towards the standing guns. Like everything else, there is a right way of doing it and a wrong way.

The first thing to remember is to keep in line abreast. Don't get in front or lag behind. Do not skirt round the thick or prickly places, for that is just where pheasants will be lurking, but go through the middle, probing the dense corners with your stick. A keeper will notice in a couple of drives which of his beaters are earning their pay and which are there for a gentle stroll in the country. You must be properly clad in a good waterproof thorn-proof jacket and trousers, hat, and have a stout whacking stick to beat the bushes. There will be a great temptation to shriek in excitement as a bird rises, and naturally you wish to warn the guns of its approach. This is generally frowned on, for shouting disturbs game more drastically than does your steadily tapping stick and may cause it to flush in numbers or to fly out of the drive. The keeper may have his own signal to warn of approaching game and, in any case, there is no room for Apache-type yells in the structured calm and careful organization of a driven shoot.

It is also tempting to comment audibly on the performance of the guns when eventually they hove into view. This is plain bad manners; a gun knows when he is shooting badly or well, and to overhear your observations on his efforts will annoy him – and with every right. I have noticed, over the years, that beaters who fall into this particular trap, and it is easy enough to do, are themselves inexperienced and would have a hard job hitting a barn if they were shut up inside it; they are, nonetheless, free enough with their advice and jests at the expense of someone having an 'off' day. The gun is a guest; the beater a shoot servant who must do his best to give the gun a good and happy day. Keep your thoughts to yourself. If people miss, try to analyse why by watching their stance and swing and by judging their timing. Those who shoot well must be watched just as closely, for one day you will find yourself in just such a position yourself and the beaters will be watching you.

Be punctual, keep a good line, listen carefully to instructions; if you are not a hundred per cent clear as to what is expected of you, ask, and do precisely what you are told. If you can keep to these simple rules, you will become a useful chap to the keeper. Age and size are no qualifications for a good beater. I have known boys of ten who beat a good deal more thoroughly and are better in every way than some men old enough to be their fathers – sometimes they *are* their fathers! The real value for you will be seeing how a keeper conducts a shooting day, having the privilege of walking through game cover on private ground, watching guns in action, learning the habits of game birds, being a small but important part

Beating is an art, and a vital part of a driven shooting day

of a team event and having the opportunity to talk to fellow-beaters about matters of guns and shooting with which your head will be a-buzz.

You will often find that some beaters are themselves experienced guns, for a true sportsman derives almost as much pleasure from beating as he does from shooting. It is not unknown for the shoot owner himself, the spouses of the guns or guns who have invited guests to shoot for them, to turn up with stick and waterproofs and join you in the line.

The opportunity to stand behind the guns is a rare one, but if it happens, then seize it with both hands. Your proper place is in the beating line, of course, but there just might be one drive in the day when they can manage without your valuable services and, if you ask politely, you may be permitted to stand back with one of the pickers-up. The picker-up waits safely well behind the line of guns and his job is to retrieve those birds which have been hit but which do not drop immediately. These are usually known as 'runners'. The gun may not be aware that the bird was touched, but it will plane down two fields back and either die immediately or run away and hide only to die miserably later. Thus, the provision of a picker-up is no more than a humane and responsible approach to shooting.

During the drive, a picker-up waits and watches, usually not starting his work until the drive is over, unless he happens to see an obvious runner scuttling towards him or landing close by. He has a perfect view of the guns, sees the birds approaching, watches the guns in action and has a good view of passing game which the

Peter lends a hand at the hare shoot.

guns have missed. When I was a lad I found it most thrilling to stand, as it were, at my private drive, 'aiming' my stick at passing pheasants and, of course, never missing one of them! One picker-up who befriended me would kindly coach me and tell me where I had 'missed' a bird and what to do to improve. Like beaters, pickers-up are usually experienced shooting men, many of whom have shot their share of game and who now prefer the different pleasures of working their dogs and taking a pride in the number and difficulty of the pricked birds they can retrieve.

If your father, mentor, uncle or other friend happens to be shooting you just might be allowed to stand with him at his peg. Some do not feel comfortable with a spectator, especially a youthful one, so you must not object if no such invitation is forthcoming. If you are lucky, you will be a privileged person with the best view of all of the business end of things. You will be told where to stand (or sit), usually directly behind the gun and close to him. The last thing he needs is to be worrying about you moving about, impeding his shooting or becoming a danger to yourself and others. He will also not appreciate any polite conversation you may feel moved to make: the state of the weather, what is happening at school or your comments on the shooting of his neighbours will be of no interest to him. No matter how jolly or friendly he is in normal life, now he is concentrating on the job in hand – you will know the feeling one day, so you must obey the Victorian directive to youngsters in general and be seen but not heard. Least of all will he thank you for advice as to how to shoot, or your views as to where he is going wrong!

Thus there are many ways in which your interest may be fed and fostered. Shooting is a long apprenticeship – some would say that it lasts until you hang up your gun for the last time as, for sure, no one can ever claim that he has nothing more to learn. There were times when strict fathers would delay the introduction of the gun for as long as possible and organize a long and laborious learning period, swinging sticks at innumerable imaginary passing birds. If, once the gun had found its way into the lad's hands, he committed but one error of safety, the weapon was likely to be confiscated for a year. Some would say that today we have strayed too far in the direction of liberality and that standards of safety as well as of marksmanship are not what they were.

The well-tried path of learning with an air rifle, getting out and about in the countryside, using your eyes and ears, talking to farmers, keepers and shooting men, reading the right books and magazines, beating and helping on shoots is a good one to follow. Shooting is about many more things than just pulling the trigger.

3
Guns

The gun is the key, the *sine qua non* of shooting, in spite of the concluding remark in the last chapter. It will become a cherished possession and even if it is replaced by a weapon of better quality it will be recollected with nostalgia. There is no gun in the world quite like your first gun, for with it you will experience moments of such exquisite joy and such acute embarrassment which are never quite the same in later life when little matters such as hitting and missing begin to assume less importance.

One myth must be dispelled straight away and that is that the .410 is the gun with which to start. More boys have suffered with these weapons, given to them by well-meaning adults, than is acceptable in a civilized society. The theory that the gun is small and light and therefore suited to youthful arms and shoulders is all right as far as it goes, but there the qualities of the weapon end. Being a small bore, it suffers from shot stringing, that is to say a long distance between the first and last pellet in the pattern which flies through the air in a long streak rather than in a close bunch. Even a 12-bore propels the shot in a sausage-shaped pattern, but in the .410 it is pronounced. The pattern, when it reaches the target, may look acceptable on the pattern plate but in real life you are shooting under a handicap. You will find those who can recall spectacular shots with this weapon, and in the days of the abundant rabbit some keepers used nothing but a .410 at this target and became deadly proficient. However, we are talking about a highly specialized and expert art, practised to a standard it is not given to many to achieve.

I have rarely, if ever, come across a youngster who could handle a .410 and yet was too small or not strong enough to handle its larger cousins, the 28- or the 20-bore. Both these guns are proper adult weapons, some use them all their lives and never progress to the 12-bore. On the continent and in America especially, the 20-bore is the traditional weapon of the driven game shooter, so it is quite possible that your first 20-bore will last you all your

A back action hammer gun – old fashioned by today's standards.

shooting career. On our shoot last year, one of our guns was suffering from pulled shoulder muscles so he turned up on the day without his usual 12-bore but with the 20-bore belonging to his son. He shot immaculately all day finding the fast handling of the lighter gun greatly to his benefit, and not a bird did he have to leave because of the few feet of range which his borrowed gun lacked.

Such considerations may be luxurious for beggars who cannot be choosers, and very often a boy has little choice in the matter of a first gun. Where a choice does exist he should go for the 20-bore or, if he is one of the well-developed lads of the 1980s, a 12-bore. Many firms, such as Parker Hale or AYA provide an excellent range of very good imported guns which are as reasonably priced as any on the market. Even that will strain father's pocket and you may have to be content with a second-hand one. If you decide to enter those shoal-infested waters, then go carefully, for second-hand guns need surveying with as much caution as horses or second-hand cars.

If you enter the second-hand market place, then the prestige of an English gun may be yours, for it is still possible to pick up an English boxlock gun by one of the honest Birmingham gunmakers for little more than the price of an imported weapon. Foreign guns have reached a high peak of quality, but the old snobbery value of an English-made (preferably London) gun holds good. We may acknowledge that the top London makers have produced the best guns in the world, but one of them will cost you £10,000 and is unlikely to come your way as a first weapon. A run-of-the-mill

29

imported gun is, to all intents and purposes, more than adequate for any demands you may make on it and, if looked after carefully, will last your lifetime and that of your son also. Still the old prejudice remains, and the English shotgun is the thing to have if you care about such matters and wish to carry your head just a little bit higher. You will not shoot any better with it, but it is pleasant to be seen with it under your arm. What you shoot well with and where it happened to have been made bear little relation to each other.

If buying second-hand equipment you deserve all you get if you go into the gunshop in the company of an inexperienced adult no matter how kind or well-meaning he may be. Even experienced shooting men can come to grief when buying second hand for there are many tricks of the trade practised by the unscrupulous, so be sure to patronize a shop with a good reputation and find someone to accompany you who knows about such matters. Old guns can be tightened in a vice, worn parts can be hammered back to fit snugly, barrels may be shortened and other shortcomings temporarily 'cured' in a way which is undetectable by any save a practised eye. It would be wrong in a book such as this to detail the snags involved in second-hand buying, for there would always be something to add to the list of caveats. 'Let the buyer beware' is a good enough motto, to which one might reasonably add, 'All is not gold that glisters'.

So we have decided that we should have a gun (anything but a .410) which is of a big enough bore to suit us. New questions come to puzzle and vex us. The single barrel, for example, which seems

A single barrel GREENER GP 12-bore: very rugged and quite good enough.

a rugged enough piece, is very reasonably priced compared with a double barrel. The answer is that there is nothing whatever wrong with such a gun, and many shooters have started their lives with one. For walking-up or wildfowling such a gun is quite adequate. 'Off the peg' single barrels tend to be full-choke. Choke is a matter I will cover in detail at the end of this chapter, but here it is enough to say that in a full-choke gun, the pattern of shot is slower to develop and is too tightly bunched for close shooting. You either miss cleanly or blast the bird to pieces. I have a single barrel which has been opened to true cylinder. I have heard of other singles which have had the last three inches of the barrel sawn off to give the same effect. This is cheaper than having choke removed by a gunsmith but it must be carefully done and the barrel may not be shortened to less than the legal limit of 24 inches.

However, the single barrel is a gun one grows out of quite quickly, for the lack of a second shot becomes more limiting the more shooting you do. As a cheap stepping-stone to a double gun it is ideal, and a good gun with which to learn. Being out duck shooting and having only one bunch of birds over your head in one flight is frustrating, if you can loose off only a single shot at them.

Some have their imaginations caught by the pump action or semi-automatic shotguns which are so popular with our American cousins. Some of these are beautifully made and sweet-shooting, but just as there is an ingrained prejudice against foreign as opposed to British shotguns, the UK shooting community has never quite taken the 'auto' to its heart. This was easy to appreciate in the days when five cartridges could be loaded so that you had the potential to shoot five birds from the same flock or five at the same bird. Now you may not load more than three cartridges at once so the accusation of an unsporting weapon is no longer applicable. Rather more relevant is the fact that the rigid construction of this type of gun makes it hard to show that it is unloaded. With a conventional gun this is easy to tell at a glance, but who knows that the 'auto' man has not inadvertently left one 'up the spout' as he clambers onto the back of a Landrover? Even with the bolt back, there is no guarantee that all is safe.

Such a weapon is not made welcome on a formal shoot, and rarely, if ever, does one appear there. This is a convention which, for better or worse, we have to accept whether we like it or not. Do not expect to be asked on many 'posh' days if an 'auto' or a 'pump' is the only gun you possess. In the pigeon hide or for wildfowling it is a useful weapon; being mostly machine made it is robust enough to handle rough work and, in many ways, is better for the job than a conventional break-action gun. I had a Brown-

Side by Side gun of the future, WINCHESTER 23 XTR with screw-in chokes, single selective trigger automatic safety, beavertail fore end, recoil pad – supplied in fitted case.

ing automatic for a short period and I used it for wildfowling. It so happened that I could not accustom myself to it after my long apprenticeship with a side by side, so I sold it after only one season on the coast with it. At the time many coastal gunners used this gun almost exclusively and their results were spectacular.

The limiting factor of full choke in the only barrel, which I mentioned in connection with the single gun, is no longer the impediment that it was. My old Browning was limited to full choke so that walked-up birds needed a good deal of 'law' before I fired. Today it is possible to vary the choke to any degree by inserting one of a series of special tubes into the muzzle. Thus you can use an improved cylinder for driven game and, in a few moments, in one simple operation, change to full choke for a duck flight.

Thus, although the automatic has its strong points, it is probably not the gun for a beginner whose only weapon it will be. It is safest to follow tradition with your first gun and go for a conventional, top-lever, double barrel. What about hammer guns? I hear you ask. Many shooting homes will have an old hammer gun lying around somewhere, the property of a long-dead ancestor, an heirloom or acquired in some rash moment as a wall-piece. All guns have hammers, of course, but those on the outside are a potential hazard, for they catch on your clothing and in the bushes: they break off when banged and a cold wet thumb on a frosty day can all too easily slip. Hammer guns are usually very old, and while in gunmaking old does not necessarily equal bad, the older any mechanical device is, the more likely it is to have suffered metal fatigue or other metallurgic ailments. Oddly enough, many of these old guns, innocent of maker's name or engraving, were once highly rated as 'good killers', and so they should have been, for they had little or no choke in either barrel. The sexton's gun of happy memory was just such a one – certainly well past its best – but no doubt it had done great slaughter in its day. In short, if a hammer gun is all you have offered, then accept it gratefully and, provided it is safe (have it checked by the gunsmith), learn to use it. There is no doubt that those brought up on hammer guns and who learned about their peculiar ways, are usually very safe and careful shots.

Another choice which has arrived to bedevil us is side by side or over and under. In the first gun, the barrels are placed side by side in the traditional manner, in the second, one above the other. Advocates of the over and under like the quicker sighting provided by the narrow rib, and this type of gun is used by almost all serious clay shooters. Those opposed to them say that they need more room to open them to clear the lower chamber (bad news in a cramped pigeon hide) and claim they prefer the traditional, broad-sighting plane to which they have grown accustomed. As for tradition, such an argument may be refuted by the fact that both Boss and Purdey, together with other 'best' makers, have, in their time, manufactured over and under guns, to buy one of which in 1985 might set you back a cool £20,000 or so. Today the very great

The over and under shotgun is popular with clay shooters.

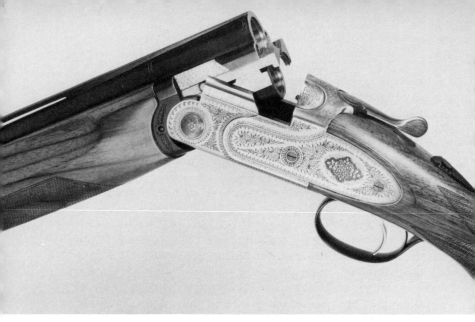

Beretta 687EL Game
O/U side-plated boxlock, single selective trigger, Automatic safety
catch, 28" barrels, ¹/₄/¹/₂ chokes, ejector, pistol grip or straight-hand
stock, double trigger – 20ga. Also in Skeet, Sporting and Trap.

majority of over and under (OU) guns are made on the continent
or even in Japan and also imported from America. Some of them,
such as Browning or Perazzi, are top quality, displaying design and
workmanship it would be hard to beat. They are expensive, but far
cheaper ones are available, and again I cite Parker Hale as one
long-established supplier of such guns.

I take no sides in the over and under/side by side controversy.
My personal preference happens to be for the latter simply
because I was brought up with one and to change at my time of life
would almost certainly be a mistake. The over and under gun is
perfectly acceptable on driven game shoots and is quite as effective
and efficient as its rival. The answer is to use what suits you best,
what you feel most comfortable holding and swinging and what
you shoot with best. If you follow that simple advice and steer
clear of the muddled arguments which flash to and fro, you will not
go far wrong.

It is one thing to decide what the ideal gun is for you, but quite
another actually to get your hands on it. I have explained that guns
are expensive things and many of us are not rich people. Some of
us inherit guns, left us in grandfather's will or passed on by a
relative who has no further use for it. This gun was not made for us
to shoot, and to try and use a weapon owned previously by a man
six feet tall with long limbs is a mistake and puts us under a great
handicap. It is as difficult as trying to look smart wearing someone

else's suit. However, if you are lucky enough to inherit a gun, it is an easy matter to have it adjusted to fit.

Sometimes generous fathers or uncles, if they have no gun of their own to give or lend, will buy you one; remember, though, to avoid the dreaded .410. If this happens you are really in luck, and the imported 20-bore or 12-bore, or maybe even an English one (if you still care about such matters) may be yours. If this is the case, then read carefully the points about the importance of gun fitting which appear later in this chapter.

A third choice is to save up and buy (or get someone to buy for you) your own gun. This is a good way to do it, as you feel you have really earned the gun, when at last it becomes yours, for it has come as the result of hard labour, and you respect and cherish it all the more for that reason. My father was in no financial position to buy me a gun, although he had provided the air rifle, so I had no option but to work on the farm during harvest. I did everything from weighing plums to pitching sheaves, saved my pay and in the autumn made my first purchase.

The gun I bought was the most unsuitable you can imagine, for almost everything I have warned about in this chapter was wrong with it. In those days there was not the expert guidance nor the range of guns available. In spite of my ghastly mistake, I was now a gun owner and have been one ever since. The shortcomings of this weapon, (a pump action Winchester 1897), may have been legion, but I cherished it dearly and shot a good many birds with it. Once you have stepped onto the ladder of gun ownership you have something with which to trade when the time comes to change it. You may not be able to afford to own two guns at the same time, but part-exchange your present one for what is, hopefully, a superior one.

In other cases, guns may be loaned by friends, kind farmers who allow you to go bird scaring, or others who may be aware of and are prepared to foster your interest. Whether your first gun is begged, borrowed or donated, be sure that you have somewhere safe where you have permission to use it, that you are familiar with the strict laws on the subject of gun ownership (see Chapter 11) and act on the equally strict laws of safety. I know you have to start somewhere, but having somewhere to shoot, undergoing an apprenticeship with airgun and beating stick and familiarizing yourself with the rules of the game ought to come before you become a gun owner. It is far easier to become the latter than to learn the former.

Before we come to the all-important matter of gun fitting, there are one or two technical terms and points which ought, for the sake of thoroughness, to be explained: boxlock and sidelock are the two most common alternative actions in standard guns. Boxlocks are simpler in design than sidelocks and are therefore cheaper, but in no way worse from a practical standpoint. The lines of the sidelocks are more graceful and there is more exposed metal on which the engraver can express himself.

Most guns have two triggers: one for firing each barrel. On an over and under gun, the right trigger fires the bottom barrel, the left fires the top. On a side by side gun, the front (right-hand) trigger fires the right barrel, the back trigger fires the left-hand barrel. Some guns specially made for left-handers may reverse the order, but there are very few such weapons in existence. Some guns have only one trigger which may or may not be selective.

The safety catch is a misnomer. Even when 'safe' is displayed, the springs are compressed and the hammers cocked. The safety catch merely immobilizes the triggers so that they may not be pulled. A gun 'on safe' might go off if dropped or jarred. The safety catch should be slid forward with the thumb as the gun is raised to the shoulder. As the gun is broken, the catch automatically returns to 'safe' except in certain guns, usually used for clay shooting, where there is a non-automatic safety catch fitted. These need special care, and if you borrow someone's over and under gun, be sure to ascertain if the safety is automatic or not. On single *selective* trigger guns, the barrel selection mechanism is usually incorporated in the safety catch. A shotgun with cartridges in the chambers is never safe, a point worth remembering.

In writing of choosing a gun, I spoke of the choke in, say, the single barrel being a limiting factor. Choke is a constriction at the muzzle which means that shot reaching it from the cartridge is bunched tightly together before it leaves the barrel. The moment the pellets leave the muzzle, they begin to disperse: the greater the degree of choke, the later this happens. Pattern is the distribution of pellets at the target so the tighter the choke, the more pellets are in that area. This can lead to missing or damaging game at close range. By the same token, too open a pattern disperses more quickly so that at longer ranges, there may be insufficient pellets in the vital area to ensure clean kills.

A standard load, 12-bore cartridge with about three hundred pellets in it will place the following number of pellets in a 30-inch circle at 40 yards' range:

True cylinder (ie least choke)	120 pellets
Improved cylinder	135 pellets
Quarter choke	150 pellets
Half choke	180 pellets

Three-quarter choke	195 pellets
Full choke (ie most choke)	225 pellets

As most sporting shots are taken well within 40 yards (35m) range it is clear that full choke is not the most efficient. It is a very tall tree indeed which is half that height and very few game birds (although not wildfowl) will fly above that height. The boring of barrels is a matter of personal choice, but it is usual to have improved cylinder in the first (front trigger) barrel, and quarter or half choke in the other. As I have explained, choke is easy enough to remove, but once it has been taken out, there is no power on earth which will put it back.

The chamber of the gun is the place where you put the cartridge and most 12-bore shotguns have chambers of 2½ inches (65mm) or 2¾ inches (70mm), and this is the length of the cartridge case after it has been fired. It is highly dangerous to fire cartridges of greater length than the chamber of the gun. For example, 3-inch cartridges are available for wildfowling guns with 3-inch chambers, but to fire such a cartridge in a 2½-inch chambered gun would be to risk a severe accident.

Only a good gunsmith can tell you whether your gun is a good fit or not. Many beginners find themselves with a gun with too long a stock, and to shoot with such a one is to operate under a handicap. The gun will be out of balance; you will be stretching to reach the triggers, suffer from cut fingers and have a generally miserable time. The gunsmith will help you determine which is your stronger ('master') eye, for you ought to be shooting from the same shoulder as your master eye. A simple DIY test to find out which eye is stronger is, in one quick movement, to point your finger at a small, distant object, keeping both eyes open as you do so. Close your right eye: if the finger and the object are no longer in line, you have a right master eye. To confirm this, open your right eye and close the left and your finger will still be in line with the object.

Some of us have eyes of roughly equal power or maybe a left eye which is occasionally, but not always, dominant. In such cases, it is better to shoot from the right shoulder, making a positive effort to 'switch on' the right eye as you mount the gun. Left-handed guns are comparatively rare and to convert fully a right-handed gun can be an expensive job. In relation to this matter is the 'cast' of the gunstock which refers to the degree to which the stock has been bent in relation to the barrels, in order to bring the barrels into alignment with the shooter's master eye. A gun is said to be 'cast on' if it bends to the left (as measured from the butt) or 'cast off' if it bends to the right.

The stock itself is usually made of walnut and is valued and appreciated for its 'figuring'. This is the natural pattern in the wood, and the degree of finish, oil or polish, which makes the stock look attractive. The shape of the hand-grip may vary from the traditional game-gun straight hand stock to a semi-pistol grip or full-pistol grip found more commonly on single barrels, on wildfowling guns and on some imported weapons. In the same way, the wooden fore-end which locks the barrels in position may be the straight, English style, or the American beaver-tail fore-end – again, this is very much a matter of personal choice.

Finally, I have mentioned the word 'bore' a number of times, and a favourite question in sporting quizzes is to ask how the bore of a shotgun is defined. The bore is measured by the number of spherical, lead balls which fit exactly into the muzzle-end of the barrel which make up 1lb weight. In other words, a 12-bore would have twelve such balls, a 20-bore twenty, and so on. Thus, the higher the number of the bore, the smaller the actual diameter of the muzzle. The largest measured in this way are 4-bores and 8-bores and they are the largest guns of all, being used almost exclusively for wildfowling.

As the owner of a shotgun, you will be meticulous in matters of care and maintenance. Your gun is an expensive investment which will deteriorate if neglected; it is less likely to break or let you down if you have looked after it and it will remain in a safe condition if regularly inspected. At the end of every season it is wise to have your gun inspected and cleaned by a qualified gunsmith; the few pounds it costs are more than well spent when set against a dangerous or irritating breakdown in the field.

Every time the gun is used it should, as a matter of strict routine, be cleaned afterwards. Old shooting men get into the habit of seeing to the needs of the dog, cleaning the gun and then seeing to themselves in that rigid order at the end of every shooting day. Modern cartridges do not deposit damaging layers of dirt beneath which corrosion and then pitting occur, so internal barrel cleanliness is not as essential as once it was. However, dirt, scratches, raindrops, an accumulation of dirt and unburned powder and good, old-fashioned mud can, if left to accumulate, seriously damage a gun. Mud is abrasive and will scratch, and finely made steel components do not function well if they are jammed with fluff – an obviously unclean and neglected gun is a very bad reflection on its owner.

Thus, a home cleaning kit must be part of every shooting man's list of essentials. This is a simple enough affair comprising a jointed, screw-together rod, a phosphor-bronze screw-in head, a wool screw-in mop, a soft-texture toilet roll, a soft rag and a tin of WD40 oil. Many old gun lists include the dreaded Turk's head brush which looks rather like a steel miniature version of a chimney sweep's brush. Do not use it. It is a relic from the days of the old fouling cartridges and is much too drastic to use on mirror-polished barrel walls.

The cleaning process is simple and here is the procedure for cleaning a gun after a wettish day in the field. Assuming you have a standard OU or side by side shotgun, remove the fore-end and reduce the gun to its three component parts, fore-end, stock and barrels. Give all surfaces a light spray with WD40 (such a boon to gun cleaners). This will remove superficial dirt and moisture and penetrate small joints and inaccessible parts of the mechanism. After a time, wipe off the surplus with absorbent tissue.

Give a good squirt of the oil down each barrel; remove dirt by pushing through a ball of toilet tissue, two sheets is about right; too little does a poor job, while too much will be tight in the bores and might cause damage when being forced through. Use the cleaning rod (I reverse it and use the handle) to push the tissues through. Repeat this process until the paper comes out clean; it may take about four operations. If there is some stubborn mark in the barrel, squirt a little oil and apply the phosphor-bronze brush. This material is softer than the steel of the barrel and, therefore, will not damage it. Remove the mark and clean with more tissue. Finally give a polish and a *light* oiling with the lambswool mop. Too much oiling is a common fault of gun cleaners; an excess in a barrel can cause a 'ring-bulge' or even a burst. Use oil as if it costs £10 per tin. Check the barrels from both ends against the light and they should be gleaming.

Take special care to remove dirt and moisture from the space between the rib and the barrels, for rust building up here is hard to detect and can ruin a gun if allowed to build up. Use the WD40 and slide a scrap of tissue firmly down the rib and you will be surprised how much dirt you will pick up from what appears to be a clean surface. Wipe clean the flats of the barrels and remove fragments of unburned powder from beneath the extractors or ejectors. A pipe cleaner or stiff wing feather is useful for this. This can build up very quickly to the extent that ejectors become ill-fitting and may even break off. Remember to wipe the muzzles, as oil and dirt are deposited there by some of your earlier barrel cleaning operations.

The stock and action should be given a series of sharp, downward shakes and this will remove a good deal of the rainwater. The WD40 is a good water dispersant and will help you to do a clean job. Wipe off mud and blood: the latter is an especially corrosive substance, and give a light oiling to all metal surfaces. If your gun has actually been dropped into mud or water, you may feel that you need to remove the plates or the locks for a more thorough cleaning. If you are in doubt, get your gunsmith to do this for you, but if you are familiar with the mechanism it is acceptable for you to have a go. There is one vital point: the screwdriver you use must be a proper gunmaker's turnscrew which fits exactly into the slot in the screw you intend to remove. An ill-fitting one will burr the head of the screw and spoil it which, in the case of a quality gun, is a serious blemish as each screw is individually made and engraved.

You may be liberal with your initial doses of WD40, but at the end of cleaning, it should all have been removed. Oil, especially some of the proprietary brands of gun oil, tends to become sticky and dry when old. Points of maximum contact and therefore of friction require the merest drop of oil. If the gun has had a serious soaking, leave it in bits, on newspaper in a warm, dry place (but on no account next to direct heat) to help to dry it out.

Oil the stock with a mixture of linseed oil and turpentine. This will protect it from the wet, give it a smooth finish and enhance the natural beauty and figuring of the wood. Remove carefully the dried mud which tends to build up in the chequering. In severe cases this may be done with a nailbrush and clean water, but usually an old toothbrush will do. If your gun is unused for some time, check it regularly and give it a wipe down with a clean, *lightly* oiled rag. Remember that human sweat, even the unperceptible amount present on the finger tips, may make indelible marks if left

Store all guns and ammunition in a safe, locked place.

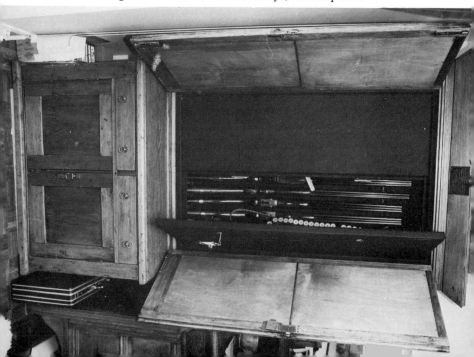

on barrels. Hold the barrels with a cloth when you put the gun away.

It is vital that your gun and cartridges are kept in a secure place. Every week one reads of guns stolen from private houses, the owners of which had been far too casual about weapon security. The recovery state of stolen guns is low, so not only is it unlikely that your treasure will be returned to you, but it might well fall into the hands of a criminal or a youngster and cause who knows what sort of horrendous accident. Gun ownership is a privilege and a responsibility, and to leave a gun easily visible on a car seat, propped in the corner of the hall or visible to anyone who may pass your house is a gross dereliction of that responsibility; others as well as yourself may well suffer, thanks to your negligence.

It may mean further expense, but it is well worth buying one of the steel gun cabinets such as those manufactured by Clayshooters Supplies Limited, of Market Harborough. These are as near to burglar-proof as one might reasonably expect, with 14-swg steel, concealed hinges, double Chubb locks and stout structure. They come in a variety of shapes and sizes and may be made to order. They are lined with baize to prevent condensation and a gun locked within is as safe as the householder may expect. There are no absolutes in matters of security, and a determined, properly equipped criminal can steal anything to which he sets his mind. Of the long list of guns regularly reported as stolen, I can think of none which have been taken from such a safe. Such a thing is a 'once only' buy, and will last for a good deal more than one lifetime.

To sum up: if you have followed all the advice, guidelines and rules I have given in this chapter, you should be the proud possessor of a shotgun. You will be familiar with the nomenclature of its various parts, understand about choke and have your gun suitably bored. You will be wary of the second-hand market but appreciate that very good guns will appear on it from time to time. Above all, you will not be afraid to seek advice from those whom you consider to be expert in the shooting world. You will know how to clean your gun and appreciate the reasons that you do so: you will have a sense of responsibility for its security and will have taken steps to store it and your ammunition in a safe place. You will know how important it is that the gun fits you well, and understand what the safety catch is for and, more important, what it does and does not do.

To possess a gun is a great and glorious thing for a beginner; to value it properly and understand it is one part of the long apprenticeship which we are calling 'Learning to Shoot'.

4
The Cartridge

Your gun is only as good as the skill you can show with it and as potent as the cartridge you put into it. An early interest in cartridges is a healthy thing and a great many lads have fostered theirs in shooting in just such a way. The shoe box under the bed with its multicoloured contents, each one a small part of gunmaking history and a reminder of some long-forgotten local gunsmith is a fascinating treasure trove. A good collection will show the gradual developments of powder from the crude black to the refined nitro powders of today. There will be cartridges of every bore from the tiniest .22-shot cartridge to the giant 1¼-inch punt-gun shell which looks as though it would be more at home in a seige gun in a battle than in a sporting weapon. The old paper cases, as opposed to the modern plastic ones, speak of the variety available to the sportsman a generation ago. For example, he could buy 8-bore ammunition from 3-inch to 4¼-inch and all sizes in between, in almost any shot size, in brass or paper. Today it is

Cartridge collecting is a popular starting point. All these are 8-bore.

impossible to buy 8-bore cartridges anywhere, for they are no longer commercially produced.

Some never give up the habit of cartridge collecting, and it is amusing to see quite old men, the light of battle in their eyes, bartering for a swap with all the fervent enthusiasm of schoolboys trading stamps. I myself, if I see a cartridge I do not possess in someone's belt on a shooting day, cannot resist the urge to offer 'one of mine for one of yours'. For those who wish to show off their collection to advantage, there is a special display board made by Cambridgeshire Gun Centre of Cambridge which does the job admirably. You fix the cartridges in place with adhesive tags, arranging them in concentric circles, chevrons or whatever shape takes your fancy: under glass and in the hardwood frame, they make an attractive show.

While collecting cartridges is a good way to familiarize yourself with the various categories of shotgun ammunition, the shooting man must also possess detailed and practical knowledge. All shotgun ammunition contains inside the case a primer which is struck by the firing pin; a measured charge of powder, wadding, shot and a crimp closure to hold in the contents. The old method of sealing the end was a card and a roll-turnover; before that they used candle-wax! The case is simply a container to hold the charge. We have seen in the chapter on guns how essential it is that the length of the cartridge (printed on the box and sometimes on each one) should not exceed the length of the chamber of the gun. The modern plastic case has the advantage of being completely water-proof, a useful thing for wildfowlers. Gone are the days of a row of damp and swollen cartridges standing, like a rank of toy soldiers, to dry in the airing cupboard. Paper cases are still made for certain game-shooting cartridges: their advocates claim that they give a better performance than plastic (an opinion yet to be definitely proven), but a definite advantage is that when they are discarded in the countryside they rot down and disintegrate, a thing which the plastic or polyethylene ones will not. It is a good habit to pick up your spent cases and dispose of them at home.

The primer cap contains a fulminate which is detonated by an internal anvil when the firing pin strikes. This, in turn, ignites the powder which, as it burns, gives off a rapidly expanding gas which, contained by the breech and the barrel of the gun, has nowhere to go but forwards. The wadding column gives a tight seal to maximize the pressure, and the gas pushes the shot out along the barrel. Any obstruction in the barrel such as mud or snow, will impede this process, cause the pressure to find another outlet, and that is how bursts or bulges occur.

43

The shot comprises a number of round pellets of lead hardened with antimony. The size of the shot varies from the tiny dust shot to the single ball or rifled slug. In increasing sizes, shot is denominated as follows: dust shot, 9, 8, 7, 6, 5, 4, 3, 2, 1, BB, AAA, SSG, SpSG, SG, LG, single ball and rifled slug. It is important to match the size of shot to the quarry species, and remember that the bigger the shot, the fewer of them for the same weight will feature in a cartridge. Some species are physically more vulnerable, and they tend to be shot with smaller shot. Remember also that the greater the number of pellets in a cartridge (ie the smaller the shot) the denser the pattern will be at optimum range.

Most game is shot with 5, 6 or 7, with 6 and 7 being the most popular. In a 12-bore this consists of 1$\frac{1}{16}$oz (30g) of pellets and it gives good patterns at the sort of ranges at which grouse, pheasant, partridge, snipe, woodcock and (most) pigeons are likely to be encountered. Some birds are tougher, have denser feathers and call for the greater shocking power of bigger shot. Thus duck might call for 3s and As while for geese you might require 1s or BBs. This leads us to the theory which supports bigger bore guns for wildfowling. The use of, say, an 8-bore for goose shooting, allows you to fire large pellets, but in a greater number than is possible in a 12-bore. In other words, you have a much better pattern with bigger shot and for big, strong birds such as wild geese which can fly over oceans, this is a desirable combination.

The range of a shotgun is limited not by the energy of individual pellets, for a single one is capable of dealing a mortal blow at double what is considered acceptable range for shotgun shooting. The magic word is pattern, and as that begins to deteriorate, the shot becomes progressively less effective. At 100 yards, the pattern will cover the side of a cottage wall, but there will be gaps in it through which a horse, let alone a snipe, might pass safely. This leads us to the essential factor of all shooting which is to avoid long-range shots. A vital skill is the ability to assess *range*, not an easy thing in open country with no trees or pylons to help your judgement. Practise judging distances from measurable objects so that you can pace out and check your guess.

Shots fired at excessive range (remember that 40 yards is a very long shot indeed) can only wound. A bird which escapes with shot in its body is likely to die a cruel and agonizing death, unless its sufferings are cut short by a predator, and is a shameful thing, unsporting, and a blot on the face of shooting. The trouble is that a fluke pellet might (by the purest chance) just happen to strike a bird in the head or a major wing bone, bringing it down instantly. The odds against this happening are long indeed, but when it does,

Pinkfeet overhead. It is vital to match the cartridge with the quarry.

the shooter and those who happen to witness the event, can so easily gain the impression that it can be done every time. Much has been said and written about shotgun range but always remember that the maximum effective range of a gun in relation to a given kind of game is the greatest range at which it is reasonably certain that a clean kill will be made by a truly aimed shot.

For a 12-bore with a standard load, the maximum effective range is 35-40 yards for general game but for stronger quarry such as mallard and wild geese this may be reduced to 30 yards. Smaller-bore guns will have a correspondingly shorter maximum range. While all bores create similar patterns, the smaller bores will throw fewer pellets into the target area, so their maximum effective range will be correspondingly less.

Some guns, you will find, throw some shot in tighter and more even patterns than others. One gun may shoot 6 shot better than 7, while the next gun bored in the same way and similar in all other respects, will shoot 7s better than 6s. A gun can be regulated by a gunsmith to shoot your favourite load most effectively, but a cheaper alternative is to pattern the gun yourself. It is a waste of time firing at a large cardboard box put on a gatepost; the test must be carried out properly. Patterns are assessed by firing no

Good patterns at close range are necessary for game shooting.

less than 6 shots from a previously fired barrel at a sheet of plain paper or, ideally, an iron plate at least 4 feet square at 40 measured yards – not paces. The plate should be whitewashed so that every pellet will make a mark. Describe a 30-inch circle by means of a crude compass; I use a 15-inch piece of wood with a nail in each end, and put a smear of mud in the centre for an aiming mark.

Fire a shot at the plate and count the number of strikes within the circle. If you can find 50% of the total shot charge from an improved cylinder barrel with a fair consistency from shot to shot, then you have no cause for alarm. Larger shot tends to give better *percentage* patterns than small shot. When you assess the pattern on the plate, you are looking for the ideal of a 'pepper-pot' pattern, one in which the strikes are distributed with geometrical regularity. There should be no ominous gaps or tight bunches of pellets; through one a bird might pass unscathed, while the other would smash it. A useful check is to have a piece of wire formed into a 5-inch-diameter circle, and see how many times it can be placed within the 30-inch circle without covering a pellet. Too many of these is clearly bad news and will mean missed or wounded game. If the test confirms this failing, then try another type of cartridge or change the shot size by *one* and hope to see an improvement. As a last resort, the borings will need to be regulated by a gunsmith. Do not become over-concerned with the matter, since, with an improved cylinder pattern of about 150 strikes, you might reasonably expect to find five or six holes the size of a small saucer, but in spite of this, this is the barrel boring and shot load which kills 90% of the game shot in the British Isles. The other popular load, 1oz of no.7, would expect to fare no better.

It is worth noting the theoretical density of the various patterns/ density of standard borings: full choke – 70%, three-quarter choke – 65%, half choke – 60%, quarter choke 55%, improved cylinder 50%. Always remember that uniformity of spread and freedom from vacant patches are far more important than precise density. Performance in the field is what counts and it can be a mistake to overfill your head with theory. Many learned books and articles have been written on this subject alone and it is possible to make a lifetime's study of it to the exclusion of practical shooting, and still be no better a marksman!

The other useful lesson of the pattern plate is whether your gun is shooting dead centre. Raise the gun and fire at the blob on the plate in one single movement, not aiming the weapon deliberately like a rifle. In this way the alignment of hand, eye and barrel can be checked. Shooting low may be remedied by straightening the stock or adding height to the comb. Shooting high can be rectified by increasing the bend, although it is no bad thing to have a gun which throws its charge well up to the mark. Stock alterations should only be carried out after careful thought and expert advice, but any competent gunsmith can do the work easily. The under-lying point of experiments with the pattern plate is to prove to the shooter that his gun shoots straight, he is aiming correctly and that his patterns are satisfactory. Once you have proved this to yourself, (or taken steps to ensure that they all happen) then you know that when you miss, the gun and cartridge are not to be blamed. Getting the gun and the cartridge right will instil confidence, and confidence is the shooter's strongest asset. Birds are not killed by guns but by charges of shot, and then only by those pellets travelling with adequate velocity, which the regularity and density of the pattern, combined with the skill of the shooter, are together capable of bringing to bear. This is all we need to know about the matter, and having ascertained how our own cartridges perform, let it rest at that.

Home-loading is an aspect of the cartridge world which has attracted a great deal of attention. Cartridges are a buyers' market at the moment with many firms seeking to undercut each other in a price war which only the consumer can win. A few years ago this was not the case, and annual price increases made cartridge buying a matter for concern. Despite the current favourable rates, there is still a saving to be made by home-loading, by means of which you may improve on the price of retail ammunition. The cartridge case is a recycled one, clean, dry and uniform in type, probably salvaged from the mountains of them at the local clay ground. Plastic is nowadays preferred to paper for reloading. The case costs you nothing, but the most expensive component is the shot, so it is wise to 'shop around' or co-operate with other reloaders to make a large bulk buy. The cost of caps (primers), powder and wadding can also be minimized by buying in quantity.

The modern, commercially produced cartridge has reached a high standard of consistency and reliability – admittedly something of a compromise to accommodate the *general* requirements of different guns in varying circumstances. Thus, as well as saving money, the home-loader is able to produce cartridges specifically suited to his own gun and his particular requirements in the field.

Reloading is not the field for amateur experiment! It is most important that the reloader sticks to a reliable manual on the subject (such as Shooting Times, *Guide to Cartridge Reloading* by David Garrard) and follows precisely the step-by-step directions. An extra pinch of this or that is the recipe for disaster. Having said that, reloading calls for no profound knowledge of ballistics nor a PhD in chemistry, for the mechanical aspects are easy to master and you should have no problems in producing ammunition which performs quite as well on game or clays as any you may buy in the shop. What is required, however, is a sensible, mature and logical approach to the business and a careful, conscious effort to get it right.

Some old-fashioned hand-reloading tools, relics of grandfather's day, are still in circulation and they work perfectly well. I have reloaded many a case on such a set and found them entirely satisfactory. The drawback is the comparative slowness of the operation and the fact that every load of shot and powder must be individually measured by hand for each cartridge. This is all rather laborious and can lead to a slight inconsistency of cartridge performance: however, it is a good way to learn about the process from the bottom.

In almost universal use is the turret type of reloading tool, much more expensive than hand tools but a once-only purchase. This type of reloader may be set to load to a specific specification and carries out every facet of the operation while on the press, without having a human hand laid upon it. Such a machine will remove the spent primer (de-cap), insert a new one (re-cap), re-size the case, insert a measured charge of powder, seat the correct wadding column, load the shot and complete with a neat crimp closure indistinguishable from a bought cartridge. At each stage the correct pressure is applied and there is a gauge to show that no mistake occurs. It is possible in an evening, with plenty of components and clean, prepared cases to hand, to load enough cartridges for a season's shooting.

I have mentioned that the machine is an expensive item, especially for a beginner, but it is quite common practice for a number of shooters to share ownership of one, each member of the syndicate having it in his possession for a few weeks in every year or, better still, everyone assembling for a series of nights on a mass-production session when sufficient reloads are made to see you all through the season.

It is important to test your reloads in the same way as you test your shop-bought cartridges. Use the pattern plate in the way I have described earlier in this chapter and vary the load (strictly according to the tables) until you have a produce which suits your gun and your type of shooting. Scan the inside of your barrels for grains of unfired powder: this is usually the sign of too weak a crimp closure for it is impossible to reproduce, in a second-hand case, the strength of the original. If you have problems with this, a dab or two of varnish is usually the answer. Reloaders who may become bitten by the 'bug' and who decide to take the matter seriously, may care to have their home loads properly tested which can be done (for a fee) at the laboratory of The Birmingham Proof House, Banbury Street, Birmingham. Consignments should be marked 'Ammunition. Class 6. Division 1. Safety Cartridges. Not liable to explode in bulk' and sent, not through the post which is illegal, but by road carrier. In return you will receive a full report on each cartridge submitted in terms of load, pressure, velocity and recoil. The Proof House will not advise on reloading matters, but only make reports on laboratory tests.

My own reloading experience comprised only hand-tool work, loading some special 3-inch magnum cartridges for coastal goose shooting, producing a good, low velocity load of good patterns. Later on, and to this day, I load my own 8-bore cartridges with black powder. I have explained that no 8-bore ammunition is commercially available. Believe me, the feeling of pride and elation you have when a bird falls to a cartridge of your own making, is one of the great thrills of shooting. It is similar to the delight a trout fisherman feels when he catches a trout on a fly of his own design and manufacture. Home-loading is itself a fascinating aspect of shooting, and one to which every aficionado is prepared to devote any amount of time and money. At its most basic, for the novice, it is the only way he can reduce his cartridge costs and, later, load ammunition to suit his specific needs.

It can be a mistake to become too much concerned with what cartridges you are using. I went through a stage of anxiety about shot-size and general ballistics until it came to the point that it was interfering with my actual shooting. On a duck marsh, for example, my various pockets held different types of cartridge, no.7 for snipe, no.5 in case a pheasant sprang from the rushes and some no.3 for the mallard. Walking out to flight, you were never certain what was about to spring from in front of the nose of the questing dog. At one point I was in the ludicrous state of having no.7 in one barrel for the snipe and no.3 in the other for the duck. In the heat of the moment, it is more than easy to fire at the wrong target with the wrong cartridge, or to carry out a rapid reloading with a completely inappropriate shell. An Indian sportsman claimed to have 7s in one barrel for bush pheasant and SSG in the other in case he saw a tiger. A mistake in those circumstances could have had serious consequences for, while a fluke pellet might have bagged the pheasant, the tiger would become very angry indeed on receiving a salute with an ounce of no.7!

I even tried keeping different types of cartridge in special sections of my cartridge belt – thus 7s on the right, 3s on the left, 5s in the middle, but still I found myself grabbing the nearest, and usually the wrong one, in the heat of the moment.

At last I saw sense and, having absorbed enough theory to get me by, I threw all of the technical data out of the window. Like many beginners I was obsessed with *range*, that false god, and hence that other charlatan *choke*. For certain sorts of wildfowling both are important, but for general, all-round game and pigeon shooting they are a handicap. The best general ammunition for shotgun shooting is a light load of no.6 or no.7 shot which will put an evenly distributed pattern within the 30-inch circle at your average range of shooting. This load will kill most of what you have the chance to address on an average day out and is ideal for those close range shots. Make sure of them and forget the tales told by old gunners of their full choke, long-barrelled goose guns, firing 2oz of BB and dropping duck and geese 'from the clouds'. It is all nonsense, a snare and a delusion.

I learned the hard way, and it was fun finding out, but I now use Eley Impax 7s in an open-bored gun for all of my general shooting and my 8-bore or Alphamax 3s for wildfowling. Not only does it make life much simpler, but at the end of the day, my bag is a good deal heavier than it was.

5
Accessories

Much of the fun in shooting or in any other sport, lies in the saving up for, choosing, buying, cherishing, maintaining and using the various accessories and appendages to the sport which the man in the shop considers are so essential. There is a rare aura, a charisma to the bits and pieces made of brass and fine grained cow-hide with which the shooter is tempted to surround himself. All you really need to shoot are a gun, a cartridge, a game-bird and somewhere to go – everything else is non-essential, but fun.

Top of the list, and something you should have from the moment you become a gun owner, is a gun cleaning kit. This will comprise a set of wooden screw-together rods, a tin of oil and a selection of screw-on appendages, rather like a miniature chimney sweeping set. In an earlier chapter we saw how to use it and how important it is in preserving the gun. If you are able to set aside a special place in the shed or workroom for a gun-cleaning corner, so much the better. An old table or bench with a piece of discarded carpet or baize stuck onto it and your cleaning tools hanging neatly to hand is the ideal set-up.

Some old hands carry their cartridges in their side pockets, which is all very well, but sometimes they are hard to get at in a hurry and tend to unbalance and impede you if you are carrying too many of them. In common usage today is the cartridge belt which distributes the weight of the ammunition round the waist but means that a cartridge is ready to hand the moment it is required. Some belts have loops closed at the bottom, others have open loops. I prefer the former as in an open looped belt, once the leather has slightly stretched, a cartridge can slip in, right down to the brass head, and become awkward to pull out. In severe cases, they have been known to fall through. Closed loops, no matter how loose they become, will suffer neither problem. I still use the one I was given on my twenty-first birthday (quite a long time ago) and it still works perfectly well and, although stretched, is has never lost me a cartridge.

A cartridge belt should not allow cartridges to fall out.

There are some patent bandoliers on the market with a species of metal clip in which the cartridge fits. I have no personal experience of these, but would be worried at scratching my gun on that bristling array of metalwork and I wonder if, with age, the springs weaken and slacken their grip. Another device holds the cartridges in a long sausage slung round one shoulder and ending in two patent release devices on the shooter's opposite hip. Again I lack first-hand experience, but I heard of one which went beserk and shot its complete contents out into the mud. Also it is impossible to tell at a glance how many cartridges you have left. With most such devices, simplest is best, and the traditional closed loop cartridge belt made of leather will last a lifetime and do all that you expect of it.

Some game shooters prefer to keep their cartridges in a hide cartridge bag. The old ones were lovely things, made of cow-hide or pigskin with brass fittings and designed by that mighty shooting man, Sir Ralph Payne Gallwey. It is hard to think that design was a feature of a simple bag, but in fact, it is all important. The webbing strap did not slip off the shoulder: when the flap was opened and bent back, it stayed open and did not close maddeningly at the most inconvenient moment. The aperture was reinforced internally with metal and was just the right size for a hand in a hurry to be thrust in. Brass fittings did not rust: the strap could be detached and replaced if necessary, but its anchoring points were at the ends of a broad leather band which ran under the bag and took the not inconsiderable weight of, say, a hundred cartridges. Look for nothing less if you should decide to buy a cartridge bag. It is still popular on some driven shoots with short distances to walk, but the rough shooter, pigeon shooter or wildfowler is usually a belt man.

It is worth mentioning in passing the cartridge magazine. This too was made of hide leather, often on oak, brass bound and massively made. Old ones are things of beauty and keenly sought by collectors. Their heyday was when a sturdy manservant might carry one behind a gun on the way to a grouse butt, or to hold a large reservoir of cartridges on a train journey to some distant shooting ground. New ones may still be bought, and there is no harm in having one in which to store your ammunition at home, but put it low on your list of priorities. They too were well designed with sections inside to hold ranks of cartridges and a series of straps to lift them up.

Another important container is the game bag. Those small ones with the netting front are all very well, but a cock pheasant crammed in one for a long day is a sorry looking object when you display it proudly back home. A game bag should be voluminous enough to hold a good head of the game you are ever likely to shoot in a day without spoiling it, with enough room for a spare sweater, a pull-through (in case of a blocked barrel), an extra box of cartridges, your lunch, torch, map and compass (for wildfowlers). It should, moreover, still have room for the mushrooms you may find or some other treasure. Something in the style of the GPO delivery satchel is ideal, and the nearest equivalent commercially available is called 'The Bag for all Seasons' which may be obtained from Shooting Developments Limited, of Fife in Scotland. Take your game bag with you on even the shortest and least promising outing with the gun. Shooting is a sport which calls for freedom of both hands at once so that if one of them is encumbered with a bird, your efficiency is severely hampered.

One way to carry birds without damaging them is in the series of miniature leather or cord lassoos which are slung from the belt. A bird's head is quickly slipped in and may be carried home without damaged tail or soiled plumage. These are good for short journeys, but for long walks the birds will swing, bump your legs and generally impede your progress. What is more, you will find blood smeared on your nice clean shooting trousers. An alternative is the pair of metal fingers, fixed in a permanent Harvey Smith gesture and attached to a webbing strap which rests over the shoulder. It is possible to carry a dozen pheasants with ease in one of these devices, but one warning – soft-necked birds such as grouse have been known to decapitate themselves when the carrier jumps over a piece of boggy ground, so this game carrier also is intended only for short journeys.

I have mentioned that the wildfowler or any shooting man whose sport takes him into hazardous places should have some safety equipment with him. His compass should be a proper marching compass and not the sort you find in a Christmas cracker: one day it might save his life when the fog comes down. The torch should be lightweight, powerful and preferably water-proof; he should, in addition, have a loud whistle such as an Acme Thunderer and, on unfamiliar ground, a large-scale map of the area.

Every shooting man sooner or later needs a pair of binoculars. Many a pricked goose has been recovered with their aid, and several good flights at duck and pigeon have resulted from careful reconnaissance. For the woodland deer stalker, binoculars are second only to the rifle in order of importance. Much of your spying is likely to be done in poor light, so a large-object lens with its generous light-gathering power is essential. Magnification should not be too high, otherwise you will encounter problems of holding steady on a distant object. When binoculars are catego-rized, two figures appear, the first being the number of times an object is magnified, the second, the size in millimetres of the object lens. Thus, a specification of 7 × 50 gives a reasonable magnification (times 7) and a large object lens (50mm). This is the ideal all-round countryman's binocular. They can be very costly, but the imported Russian glasses called Helios are sturdy and as cheap as you will find. Many professional woodland stalkers use them. This, like much of your equipment, is a once-in-a-lifetime buy and a purchase which you are likely never to regret or repeat.

Another important item is some form of protection for the gun. For travelling any distance in a motor vehicle, a rigid motor case is essential. This holds the gun in its component parts and is stout enough to resist a very severe impact without damage. Better quality guns often come complete with a fitted motor case. Traditionally these are made in a style similar to the cartridge magazine: hide leather on oak, lined with baize with brass locks and fittings. The gun fits neatly into the sections inside and there is room for a rudimentary cleaning kit, snap caps and other useful tools. Leather gun cases are expensive but there is an alternative made of a synthetic material which is very tough, lined with foam rubber. This type is much less expensive than the traditional case which, like the magazine, is becoming something of a collector's piece, especially where the original prestigious trade labels are still attached.

For moving about on the shoot, on shooting-day transport, on the highway or at any other time when you have the gun but are not likely to be actually shooting, a slip case is required. This will not prevent the gun from being damaged by a severe blow but it will keep off the mud and prevent superficial scratches and rain water. On a formal driven shoot, it was the old custom to keep the gun in its slip until you arrived at your peg and replace it the moment the drive was over. This may no longer be standard practice but it is a good habit to adopt. May one assume that a gun in a slip is unloaded and safe? In theory, no, but gun accidents tend not to happen when weapons are so carried.

Many gunslips are made of leather, and while man-made material or canvas does the job just as well, the more expensive leather is a nicer thing to own and seems to improve with wear and age. Slips which open at the butt end only can be responsible for wearing the blueing off the muzzles. Some slips have allowed for this and feature full- or three-quarter-length zips which prevent any such friction. The strap, as with all shoulder straps, should be a non-slip material such as webbing. A leather one will slide off the shoulder at every other step, especially on a wet day. Another tip for a strap on a gun slip is to have it attached to the flat side rather than the leading edge. This prevents the gun from flapping loosely from side to side, even more so if it is carried muzzles down.

On the continent they have the custom of having sling swivels and a sling attached to the gun itself. This is not popular in the UK although it does have certain advantages for wildfowlers. Much of our general reluctance stems from a fear of spoiling the lines of a good gun, by screwing machine-made attachments onto it.

A minor but useful accessory which has become almost a cult in itself, is the thumbstick. This will be useful in many ways and on many occasions in the shooting field or just generally out in the countryside. Properly used, it can serve as a 'third leg' during long periods of standing, is essential for beating, useful for the picker-up, a depth of mud and water tester for the wildfowler and handy companion on country walks. Some sticks are works of art, delicately carved in ramshorn to represent any number of subjects but calling for many hours of careful work to produce. Stag horn is cheaper, but there is any variety of materials, shapes and woods used. A 'best' stick can cost a small fortune to buy but a good countryman prefers to make his own, cutting it when the sap is down in winter and carving or polishing as necessary to suit his height. A best stick ought not to be used for beating and bashing down thick brambles, or it will be ruined in a matter of a few hours.

No shooting man or any country person ought to go out without a pocket knife. Time was when a knife, together with string and a sixpenny piece, featured in the pockets of every self-respecting boy in the land. A wide variety of knives is available, many of them the lock-blade sort which cannot close accidentally and painfully on the fingers of the user. In my view, the high carbon, extra hard steel which looks so smart is very difficult to sharpen. Softer steel is best, and since a good many knives end their days lost or left behind somewhere, it does not do to spend much money on one. A cheap, soft steel knife such as the Opinel costs about £2 and is ideal; it is not the end of the world should you lose it, and it may be whetted to razor sharpness on the nearest piece of rock or doorstep. Another good knife, but rather more expensive, is the Swiss Army knife which, with its multitude of gadgets is almost a complete workshop in itself, although I believe that the device for extracting stones from horses' hooves is now considered obsolete!

There are some beautiful stalking knives to be had, but the fear of losing one is enough to prevent the owner from ever taking it out of doors. A knife need not be large to be effective. The fearsome dirk slung from the belt has few practical uses and is more likely to draw unkind attention to the wearer. Many a great stag has been gralloched with nothing more than a single-bladed, sharp penknife.

Worth mentioning, if only for the sake of being thorough, is the shooting stick. This tends to be the province of the shooter of senior years and need not concern the beginner. An interesting feature of shooting sticks is that, like knives, they have a habit of being left behind by their owners here and there about the countryside.

Often in your shooting career you will find a hide useful; this is especially true of the wildfowler and pigeon shooter. The best hides are those you make from the natural materials, grasses and bushes, that grow in the place where you intend to lurk. Quite often, due to the very nature of the terrain or the time of year, a portable hide is necessary. Basically this is a simple enough affair which, at its crudest, is four sticks surrounded by netting intertwined with leaves or scraps of green and brown cloth within which the shooter crouches. Problems arise when the ground is too soft or too hard so that the sticks sink in too deep or not deeply enough to support the weight of the net. A shooter requires a high backdrop to conceal his outline as he rises to shoot, so poles of varying heights are called for.

The best poles are lightweight and telescopic with a spike on the bottom to penetrate hard soil, and a 'foot' to prevent it from falling over. At the top should be a V-cut, onto which the meshes of the net may be hung. Parsons of Nailsea in Gloucestershire make an excellent set of hide poles which have their own special webbing, carrying strap and sling. These have all the right qualities, being made of aluminium and finished in a non-reflective matt green. It is not difficult for the technically-minded to make a set which is not only fun, but cheaper. A hide is usually best situated with its back to a bush or woodside in such a way that the backdrop is provided for you, leaving you to build up the front only with your net and poles.

The ready-made net itself may be bought with the strips of rot-proof camouflaged material already attached and of an overall size to suit your needs. West Dorset Nets of Bridport make good ones, especially the one in light coloured rather than dark material. In my opinion, many hides are coloured too dark so they have the opposite effect to that which the shooter intended, making him more rather than less conspicuous. Just examine the setting in which the hide is to be built; the predominant effect is of young corn, stubble, bleached rush, dead grass – all of them pale rather than dark colours. Lovat green and deep brown occur rather more infrequently than you might think.

A good net should be waterproof, otherwise it will absorb rain water, become heavier by degrees and gradually pull over the poles. The poles may be guyed for extra stability, but you still have to carry many pounds weight of sopping-wet net home with you. It is quite easy to make your own camouflage net. All you require is a section of netting such as an old tennis or cricket stop net, or a net such as gardeners use to keep birds off soft-fruit bushes. Hang it on the clothes line and thread through the meshes as many pairs of ladies' discarded nylon tights or stockings as you can beg. Some of these may be dyed various shades of green in Drummer dyes. The result is a lightweight net which you can see through without yourself being seen: it absorbs not a drop of rain, may be as large or as small as you like, and coloured to suit your own type of shooting background. It costs almost nothing and lasts indefinitely. Its worst enemy is the bramble and the blackthorn which will, unless you are careful, tangle it up inextricably.

Often used in conjunction with the hide is the decoy. These fall into two main categories, pigeon decoys and wildfowl decoys. A decoy is a model of a bird, a number of which may be placed in lifelike, natural attitudes to draw quarry species within range of the gun. We shall learn more of the technique of deploying decoys in the sections of this book devoted to pigeon shooting and wildfowling. The basic requirements of all decoys are fairly obvious. Most of all, they should bear a close resemblance to the birds they represent. A pigeon has white wing flashes and collar; these are recognition signals which all gregarious birds have in various forms and so they are an essential feature. There was a time when pigeons could be decoyed by the crudest of caricatures, but today the bird has grown wise to clumsy imitations so only the best will do. Some decoys, such as Shell decoys, represent the outline of a feeding bird of the correct colour and with all the right recognition signals and these work well. Other choices are full-bodied birds made either of rubber or especially tough and lightweight material called polymer, or – a favourite with many experts – a dead pigeon with its head propped up on a piece of wire.

Decoys often need to be carried for long distances so it is important that, as well as being realistic in appearance, they are not heavy or bulky to carry. Shell decoys (goose and pigeon) have the advantage that one fits inside another, so that twenty take up no more room than two. Polymer, the other popular material, is light but bulky, so the decoyer will probably need a sack in which to carry enough for a reasonable shoot, no less than a dozen for wildfowl or pigeon, but the more the better. Some rubber decoys

Goose decoys: the shell model is effective. Keep a good distance between them.

are inflatable and so combine lightness with little bulk and there are several other variations on the same themes. Decoys, like much other shooting paraphernalia, tend not to be cheap, so buy a set to last a long time, which, if you take care of them, they will do.

Our American cousins have made a special study of calls which attract various creatures to within range of the gun. In the UK this remains an under-explored area, over-ripe for development. Calling is an art and a field craft in itself and requires a good knowledge of the ways of the quarry species. Calling may be used with any gregarious, vocal species such as duck and geese, to attract a predator by means of the cry of a potential victim, or more rarely, to attract a creature by use of its mating call. The old timers used whistles to call peewits to their nets, a practice now against the law, but it proves that even a generation ago the wise wildfowler knew the value of the call.

Gamekeepers will often use the high-pitched scream of a rabbit in distress to attract a stoat, marauding fox or rogue cat. This can be very effective at certain times of year and, if properly used, is an excellent aid to gamekeeping. Mallard and wigeon, like most wildfowl, are talkative birds and what sounds like a happy gathering of their brethren on the water below, especially when the deceit is compounded by use of a few decoys, can be a certain draw. Mallard calls are many and varied, the OLT, the Marshland and the Lohman, all imported from America, being among the best with the OLT 66 as my personal favourite. It is one thing to be the owner of a duck call, but quite another to know how and when to use it. The call should only be blown at specific passing birds, which fly by in ones and twos: calling big flocks is a waste of time, as is blowing optimistically at empty wastes of open sky. A wigeon call can be made by hammering two brass cartridge case heads into each other; ideally these should be long brass cases and you have to fit one carefully inside the other, or, more simply, tape two ordinary cartridge cases together. In both cases you knock out the two firing caps. You can also buy a proprietary call or even use the whistling part from a whistling kettle. As usual, the things which you yourself have made will give the most pleasure.

Geese may be called by an imported call such as the excellent Marshland from America (available from Ralph Grant and Son), or by mouth. Mouth calling is a special skill, mastered with practice, and a speciality of some of the more famous old wildfowlers such as the late Mackenzie Thorpe of Sutton Bridge. Geese may be called by giving the imperious 'Come here' call of an old gander, or by the gutteral, feeding buzz – both may be made with the same call.

Some roe stalkers use a call to imitate the sweet, high-pitched whistle of that delightful deer. This may mimic a territorial claim, a mating call, or the cry of a youngster in search of its mother. It is fair to say that some experienced stalkers have little faith in calling, while others swear by it.

A handful of calls of various sorts are interesting features in the shooter's list of accessories, a small part of the mystique of the sport, but, generally speaking, you may not find them the magical bag-fillers you have imagined. On their day they may make the difference between failure and success, but often the most fun you have with them is blowing them to amuse your friends!

A more practical accessory and one I would urge every field sportsman to have from the day he takes up his sport until the time when, in his old age, he finally abandons it, is a game diary. Few things give more pleasure than browsing back in such a book and recalling enjoyable expeditions which the passage of time may have made hazy. As a youthful, fledgling shooting man, I was advised to start a diary of my outings with the gun; later I extended the brief to include fishing. Now I have filled two large leather-bound books and in a moment I am able to recall the half-dozen pigeons I shot in a spinney in 1960, or precisely identify the date on which I shot my first goose. Even those 'unforgettable' days grow dim after a few years, and much of the pleasure in our sport lies in recollection.

The mallard call can be a deadly lure.

Several gun shops will sell you, at great expense, an old-fashioned game register. This is good for a shooting estate which requires simply the cold, statistical evidence of bags made over the various seasons, and the guns who were present on the day. The 'Remarks' column which I think is the most important, is a pathetic space with room for only the most parsimonious of observations. Another problem for the amateur shooter or private individual is the amount of wasted space, even in the small amount of room such books provide. For example, the numbers of red stags, capercaillie, ptarmigan or pink-footed geese one is likely to shoot in a year are likely to be few, especially in your early days. Even those favourably placed will not find their bags overflowing with such quarry species, while most of us might go through a shooting lifetime without so much as seeing one, let alone bagging it. However, each one has its full quota of columns, faithfully taking up vital space in the book, space destined to remain forever blank.

Far more satisfactory and cheaper is to buy a stout accounts book from an office stationery shop. It should be substantial as it is intended to last many years and receive a good deal of handling. Who knows, but in time it might become a family heirloom to be pored over lovingly by grandchildren, so a soft covered exercise book will clearly not do. The accounts book gives you complete freedom to draw out as many columns and to use as much space for each outing as you like. I have evolved a system which works for me and I recommend it as a method of record keeping which is quick to complete, but has plenty of room for all the necessary information.

Divide a double page of the book into Date, Those Present, Bag, Place (on the first page) and Remarks on the second page. At the top of each page the year should be boldly written to provide a quick reference when checking back. The bag column is a simple list of what was shot, while under Remarks, which I feel is the meat of all sporting diaries, I will record the hen-harrier which flew over, a right and left, a boy's first bird, where you had lunch, the excesses of the weather, an eventful journey, some interesting or unusual dog work, all the little, inconsequential things which are easily forgotten, but which go to make every shooting day a unique experience. There is plenty of room to stick a few photographs, a sprig of heather or a feather. I stick my few woodcock pin-feathers in my book rather than in my hat. You may take up as little or as much space for a day as you like. It is also important and interesting to record those days, of which there will be many, when you come home with little or nothing in the bag.

Ten pheasants in 1951 sounds much the same as ten pheasants in 1981, so you are looking to record things seen, shots missed or spectacularly hit, the interesting people present, the humour and excitement of a day with the gun. I urge you to buy and start your shooting diary the same day that you aspire to your first 'proper' gun. Its acquisition may be the first entry.

There are other things which may be loosely humped together under the title Accessories which are really peripheral to the main business of shooting, but which, maybe, will sometime come your way. The ubiquitous hip-flask, favoured by more senior shooters, may turn up in a Christmas stocking, but in my view shooting and alcohol don't mix. Position finders for making the draw on a driven shoot, old brass re-loading equipment, a metal device which you may use to record the number, position and species of the birds you have killed at a stand (a 'Norfolk liar'), pocket game record, snap-caps (dummy cartridges to fire in your gun to prevent damage to strikers and ejectors) and suchlike gew-gaws may only be described as non-essential. Unlike fishing, shooting calls for comparatively few extras; it is a mistake to burden yourself with too many bits and pieces when you set out. It is equally disastrous to find yourself miles from home and lacking a vital accoutrement.

6
Clothing for the Shooter

When learning to shoot, clothing for the job is low on the list of priorities. Anything warm, comfortable and waterproof will do. Many an otherwise enjoyable day has been spoiled by the sportsman's suffering from cold or wet. As time passes, and you begin to associate with other shooters, you will become aware that as well as practicalities, there are conventions which have to be observed. It would be inappropriate to turn up for a driven grouse shoot in warm sunshine, wearing jeans and a tee-shirt, as it would be foolish to go flighting on a saltmarsh in January wearing the same kit. Clothing is not cheap to buy, and there is a great deal of variety available. It is a mistake to spend your hard-saved money

Clothing should be comfortable and not too tight.

on unsuitable clothing the shortcomings of which you discover only after you have bought it.

Most game shooting takes place in autumn and winter. In the UK we enjoy a climate noted for its unreliability and frequent cruelty; much of a shooting day might be spent standing or crouching in the same place. These three facts make warmth high on the list of priorities, so I will start with the basics – underwear. In the old days it was red flannel, wool or the old-fashioned pyjamas which the shooter wore next to his skin. These have mercifully been superseded by thermo-insulated material such as that made by Damart. This retains the body heat and ensures a layer of warm air round the body. Damart High Force long-sleeved vests and long johns are excellent for the wildfowler or winter shooter, being almost too warm on some occasions, while they might prove to be life-savers in a savage blizzard. They need frequent washing, but be careful, they can shrink drastically if subjected to violent treatment on wash day.

Some ex-Army shops keep stocks of the old-fashioned long johns or combinations; a saltmarsh is not the place for the fashion-conscious. This clothing is made of pure wool and is warm, but not as warm and long-lasting as the modern material.

Socks should be snug and fit comfortably in the boot – there is nothing like sore feet to sour a day out. Wear a light pair of ankle socks next to the skin and over them a stout pair of shooting stockings made of a wool-and-nylon mixture – these are both warm and hard-wearing. Elastic garters or cord ties will do to keep them up. If wellingtons or waders are to be worn, seaboot stockings of white, oiled wool such as deep-sea fishermen favour are excellent. On some days there is nothing which will guarantee warm feet – the extremities of the body are always the first to suffer, but it is worth doing your best to keep the worst of the cold at bay. Shooting stockings (usually worn with breeks or plus-twos) should be of sober hue – as should all your visible shooting clothing – so beware of the bright red stockings worn by climbers and mountaineers. Tights are also useful, especially the green lisle ones, for they have no gaps through which the cold can leak in. They may be worn over long johns. Nylon tights may also be worn over your stockings and they will save a good deal of wear and tear.

Gloves play an important part in warming those other vital extremities, the fingers. How can a shooter remain manually dextrous if his fingers are so frozen that a firm thumb on the safety catch or a forefinger, precise and delicate, on a trigger is impossible? The answer is that he cannot, and he is just as inefficient if his fingers are muffled in thick, woollen gloves. The problem is not as insoluble as it might sound. The bare fingers are best for shooting, so the dodge is to warm the blood supply immediately before it reaches them. Thus the sheepskin or fur wristlets are reputed to work, for they warm the wrists so that the hands enjoy the secondary benefit. For normally cold days this might be the answer, but not in a windy, sub-zero January when the problem must be solved by a resort to the old childhood favourite, mittens.

Mittens operate on the principle that the backs of the hands and fingers up to the knuckle are protected, so the all-important fingertips retain a semblance of warmth. The woollen Millarmitt, double knit with non-slip, string palms is an old favourite, cheap enough to buy, moderately hard-wearing and available in tasteful green or brown. They have thick wrists which are vital on all gloves, and many years of using them have convinced me of their usefulness.

Another popular mitten is the sheepskin, leather hand-back with finger loop and knitted, elasticated wrist band. This protects the vulnerable back of the hand, leaving the palms and fingers free for a positive grip. On really cold days, I have worn these mittens as well as Millarmitts and have been all but comfortable.

Damart Double Force undergloves are very warm and still thin enough to allow freedom of movement and sensitivity of the fingers. They are not waterproof so should be worn only on dry days. Any gloves, or other clothing for that matter, becoming soaked and forming an outer layer, can have the effect of cooling the body more quickly than bare flesh. Woollen gloves which are steaming are doing the exact opposite to what the wearer intends.

My own favourite these days is the full, long wristed glove, either woollen with leather palms or all leather with a gap in the knuckle part of the trigger-finger. It takes a fraction of a second to slip out the finger when a shot presents itself while the hands are protected at all other times. When worn in conjunction with hand-warmer pockets which now feature in so many shooting coats, you have come as close as possible to solving an insoluble problem.

A woollen scarf is a handy thing, either worn loosely to protect the back of the coat collar or tied tightly to prevent warm air from escaping from within the protective outer layer of clothing. Old fowlers out in especially bad weather would wear an ordinary towel in this way and prevent that fearful icy trickle between the shoulder blades which does its best to spoil the most promising day out. The ex-army camouflaged, cellular netting neckcloth is popular with pigeon shooters and a useful item in the all-round shooter's wardrobe. Conventions of the formal day call for a collar and tie, an anachronism I, for one, would be happy to see die. A tie is a most inconvenient and useless thing on a shooting day, but it needs a bold man to be the odd one out. There are people who feel that a wool tie worn with a flannel shirt does help to keep in the warmth. I am not one of them and feel the best neck protection of all is the towelling cravat of the type made by Cambrian Flyfishers. This is no more or less than what its title suggests, but it is smarter than a bath towel, comes in a choice of three colours and is appropriate wear on the most important big day and also for a muddy solo outing to the marsh.

Working outwards we come to the shirt. The old adage was that wool was best, and it is still true to say that natural materials are better near the skin than man-made fibre which may be more hard-wearing and smart, but is also a cold and unkind material, especially when wet. Good shooting shirts are Viyella or Clydella, not all that hard-wearing, especially for those with bristly necks, but very warm, soft and comfortable. There is a fine new range of brushed cotton moleskin shirts, also from Cambrian Flyfishers, which are also first class and cheaper than Viyella. A good shirt should have a long, old-fashioned 'tail' and should be generously cut to allow the wearer freedom of movement and no 'binding'.

The layer between the shirt and the top coat is an important one. The principle of keeping warm is based on the building up of layers of material which conserve body heat, not allowing it to escape, but at the same time, not so bulky as to deny the wearer freedom of movement. This is especially important for the shooter who needs to be able to swing his arms, mount his gun and walk long distances. In my young days one built up the layers with old rugby jerseys, woollen sweaters, leather jerkins or ex-RAF flying jackets. The result of this was one very corpulent fowler for whom raising his arms above his head was an impossibility. Luckily, the development of body insulation, hastened by Arctic exploration, mountaineering and the space age, has reached a high standard. The quilted bodywarmer is now in almost universal use; its many panels filled with special warmth-retaining granules, better even than duck down, combine lightness, lack of bulk and allow complete freedom of movement. It comes with long sleeves or sleeveless, with vee neck or high collar, with zip or, more usually, stud fastenings.

A quilted jacket should be long enough to protect the whole of the back and fit neatly, and it should not be too tight or too loose. On a dry, bright day, such a jacket may be worn as a top coat, and is very popular with horse riders. Those made by the firm Puffa have a rip-stop nylon outer skin which makes them more rugged than the plain bodywarmers. During the last ten years, a coat such as this has become standard wear for many farmers and outdoor people as well as field sportsmen.

To protect the nether regions, old-fashioned styles and materials take some beating. Corduroy and tweed are both good, and another old favourite is brushed cotton known as moleskin. Trousers are quite acceptable for many shooting occasions, but sooner or later you will find that a pair of breeks or plus-twos will be necessary. These are standard wear for the formal shoot, but the reinforced knees and seat, the button-down pockets and the fact that they end at the knee and so make for no uncomfortable folds of cloth jammed into the wellingtons are all good design features. Good breeks are able to withstand a good deal of rain and rough passage through the prickles and are comfortable to wear, while the loose layer of cloth over the knee prevents chafing. So good breeks are an excellent, all-round shooting garment, and if at first you may feel a little self-conscious in them, you eventually reach the stage of feeling uncomfortable when not wearing them.

Again we find ourselves turning to Cambrian Flyfishers of Trevor in North Wales for an excellent range. This firm can supply most of the shooter's sartorial requirements at a reasonable cost but with high quality. Their Ratcatcher range of breeks is excellent. For really cold days you may wear a pair of quilted undertrousers, but usually the long johns plus breeks will be more than adequate. The exception is in really wet weather or when beating through especially ferocious cover when you need a pair of waterproof overtrousers. A good waterproof coat keeps dry the upper body, but sheds water straight down onto the breeches. Waterproof trousers will ensure that it continues its downward journey onto the wellingtons. Overtrousers which are proof against thorn as well as water will prevent your breeks from being spoiled by a continuous battering from the brambles, for stout as they may be, there is no cloth which will stand up to that sort of punishment for long periods.

Overtrousers should end well above the ankle or they catch on every protruding branch; they should have a stout draw-cord at the waist and full protection behind and at the sides. Those made in the cutaway style leave gaps which, while they allow cooling air to circulate, can also allow water in, especially if the wearer adopts certain postures, such as sitting down. The ankles should have zips; nothing is worse than hopping about in a hideous *danse macabre* on one leg, growing red in the face and trying to remove your waterproofs at the end of the day. The zip allows you, while still wearing boots, to slip your overtrousers on and off easily. A lining of some sort absorbs condensation and helps keep your breeches clean. A good pair of waterproofs will last many years if cleaned, reproofed and generally cared for, so it is wise to buy the right sort to start with. Some shooters prefer waterproof leggings; these have their uses and are cheaper than the full trouser, but I prefer the latter for the all-round protection and peace of mind which comes with being 100% waterproof from head to toe.

The most expensive item of shooting clothing and therefore the one which you must buy most carefully, is the top coat. On cold or wet days, the waxproof, thornproof coats of the type made famous by Barbour, or Sporting Developments International have become almost standard wear, not only for shooting men but for the many outdoor folk. They have reached an advanced state of design and now there is little to choose between them, but one or two important points must be made. Your local shop may carry only one or two different brands so, again, you may have to shop around.

The cloth is fairly standard, being waxed Egyptian cotton, heavily proofed, very strong and, when new, completely waterproof. It is important that you choose the right weight of cloth which varies from the comparatively lightweight to the heavy duty:

Three examples of properly dressed shooters.

most shooters seem to go for the latter. Length also varies, and my advice is to buy a long one which comes well over the thighs. The midriff, where your clothing meets, is a vulnerable spot and can be exposed when you stretch or bend. The coat should have a high collar which stays up when you want it to and which is a good protector from a cold, back wind. A hood is usually provided, but make sure that it is and that the fastenings are rugged enough to stand rough wear: mine seem to keep coming undone.

Pockets should be deep enough to hold some cartridges and other personal belongings: a small breast pocket is useful for your shotgun certificate and other documents which you prefer to keep clean. All pockets should have deep flaps to keep out the weather; some have fold-over 'storm-proof' tops which also help. The deep, inside game pocket, known as a hare pocket or a poacher's pocket seems now to be standard. In my view its use is strictly limited, but you never know when you might need it.

Storm cuffs are handy as they prevent blown rain from driving up the sleeves. A lined coat is generally better than an unlined one for this type of clothing tends to create condensation within it. A lining will soak up much of this. For coats which are to double as fishing coats, an unlined few inches known as a drip strip at the bottom prevents water from seeping up when you are wading.

All waxproof garments must be hung up to dry and mudstains must be sponged off. Mud is a pure abrasive agent and is death to all clothing if left. Re-proofing may be done with a tin of special wax which you paint on and rub into a warm, dry coat. Most firms offer a repair and renovation service from which the oldest coat returns as good as new.

The traditional Norfolk jacket shooting suit is a thing of beauty and is still available. It is good in fine weather, but not so suitable for the depths of winter. The good point of the jacket is the gussetted back which allows you to swing the gun freely without lifting on your arms the whole weight of the coat and its pocket contents as you do so. This factor should be noted in any coat buying you may undertake. However, a wax-proof coat and a pair of breeks (with or without overtrousers) will pass muster on any shooting day from the most casual to the highly formal. Not only are they the most comfortable and practical, but they meet the most rigorous conventions of the shooting field.

Good boots are very important. Traditional leather shooting boots are smart and comfortable, especially the modern silicon impregnated boots made by Golden Retriever. With stitched-in tongues they keep out the water, provide a good grip and ankle support. A hosepipe and a brush are all you need to keep them clean. However, unless you intend to have two pairs of boots, long rubber wellingtons alone will serve all your needs. Green Hunter wellingtons or the excellent Derriboots are a vast improvement of the old, heavy, black shapeless things which once masqueraded as wellingtons and which wore out a pair of socks in a day. Modern ones fit human feet, are light in weight and tough. A stockinet lining absorbs much of the condensation, the grip is adequate and they call for virtually no maintenance. They have fairly short lives if used heavily in rough country, and you may need a new pair every two years or so, but I cannot envisage any shooting man without a pair in his locker, so it is a price he must grin and bear. For small holes and punctures, Shooting Developments Limited of Fife, make a handy repair kit for rubber boots, and another for waxed thornproof coats. Either or both will make a handy stocking filler at Christmas.

The wildfowler will find that ordinary wellingtons are too short. He finds himself wading across flooding creeks or out onto freshwater flashes to set his decoys. When stationary, his common stance is one of kneeling in mud behind some sparse scraps of vegetation. Short wellies are hopeless in these cases, and a fowler with wet feet or muddy knees is not a happy man. Thigh boots or waders are the standard fowling wear. Green Keenfisher and Streamfisher (the former with studded soles, the latter without) are good, fit well and are light in weight. However, they are not cheap, and fowling waders tend to suffer a hard life. I do make an exception here, and use black, industrial waders which are half the price and twice as thick as the smart green ones. My current pair has seen me through eight seasons of hard work and are good for three more. Buy them from the local agricultural warehouse, but hang them up carefully by the feet and out of the direct sunlight when not in use. Sunlight and being left in folds and creases is ruination to waders and they work their evil in a surprisingly short time. Patent clips or hooks may be bought for hanging them properly.

By now, you should be fully dressed with the sole exception of the hat. The hat is one area where the shooter is permitted to express his personality, reflect the shape of his face or do very much as he wishes. Convention and practicalities demand that a hat of some sort should be worn on a shooting day. For the pigeon decoyer or duck flighter or anyone who expects the birds to come to him and not vice versa, a hat with a brim is essential. Bare human flesh, even when concealed within a hide, stands out very clearly to approaching birds, the face and hands appearing as pale blobs against a dark background. Nothing turns birds away more quickly than the pale full moon of a human face suddenly looming over the brush. A brim allows the shooter to watch oncoming birds without lifting his face until the moment of raising the gun and firing, by which time it is too late for the bird to take evasive action. Cloth cap or wide-brimmed, floppy bush hat are adequate for the purpose.

A hat will also protect the wearer from the weather and help to keep him warm; the loss through the head of body temperature amounts to 70%, so a hat will make all the difference to your comfort on a bitter, January day. A good, stiff brim will deflect the water away from your face and neck and down onto the water-proof coat. A deerstalker has tie-down flaps (as immortalised by Sherlock Holmes) and keeps the ears warm. A balaclava helmet, often favoured by wildfowlers, can be rolled up or down depending on the weather and a good woollen one will keep out a great deal of rain, especially when worn in conjunction with the hood of a waxproof coat.

There are many styles of traditional shooting headgear, including the fore and aft (for the aquiline), the pork pie (for the round-faced), deerstalker, stocking cap, camouflaged bush hat and the general purpose, old standby accepted everywhere, the ubiquitous, classless, practical but no longer cheap cloth cap. A

Ear protection is highly recommended for all shooters, not only clay men.

hat will, in time, cease to be a simple item of clothing and will assume the significance of a talisman or a good luck charm. The older and more patched the hat, the more frayed its edges, the more curious stains that appear upon it, the greater its value to the wearer. Some shooters use the hat as a repository for their various club badges or a showcase for their woodcock pin-feathers, a small but perfectly harmless piece of showmanship. Some of us come to be recognized from afar by our hats, long before the face can be identified. To lose a hat is a tragic occurrence, and I have known shooting and fishing men retrace their steps for many an hour as they search, with the aid of a dimming torch, for a treasure left on the river bank. If you want to get ahead in shooting, get a hat! When you choose a hat, take care: you may be choosing a companion for life.

The modern shooter is very well served by the clothing manufacturers and is often spoiled for choice. The old-timer had to do the best he could with his old gardening togs, india-rubber and golfing suit. Mallory and Irving made their famous climb of Mount Everest wearing little more than Norfolk tweed shooting suits and cloth caps, a far cry from the amazing foul-weather gear available now. In grandfather's day boots and coats which could be guaranteed infallibly 100% waterproof simply did not exist.

The choice now available emphasizes the need to shop carefully and find what you want for the best price, for it is a buyer's market and likely to remain so for many years. Clothing is not cheap, but buy the best you can afford because you 'get what you pay for' in this as in other things you buy. Once you have obtained the necessaries, take care of them. Keep them clean, stored on coathangers in warm dry places, repair damage as soon as it occurs, and your equipment will last you twice as long as if you neglect it.

In this chapter we have looked at the basic principles of clothing for shooting. The blend of practicality, conventions, natural materials where possible and common sense is the one at which to aim.

7

How to Shoot

A Father's Advice to his Son

If a sportsman true you'd be,
listen carefully to me

Never, never let your gun
pointed be at anyone;
that it may unloaded be
matters not the least to me.

When a hedge or fence you cross,
though of time it cause a loss,
from your gun the cartridge take,
for the greater safety's sake.

If 'twixt you and neighbouring gun
birds may fly or beasts may run,
let this maxim e'er be thine:
FOLLOW NOT ACROSS THE LINE.

Stops and beaters oft unseen
lurk behind some leafy screen;
calm and steady always be:
NEVER SHOOT WHERE YOU CAN'T SEE.

Keep your place and silent be:
game can hear and game can see;
don't be greedy, better spared
is a pheasant than one shared.

You may kill or you may miss,
but at all times think of this:
all the pheasants ever bred
won't repay for one man dead.

Commander Mark Beaufoy

SAFETY IN THE FIELD

I have never witnessed a fatality in the shooting field, but I know those who have. I have seen one or two random pepperings, odd pellets and there have been countless occasions when an accident has been narrowly averted or when, had a gun gone off at a critical moment, a death or a ghastly wound would have resulted. Shotgun accidents tend to be rare, and this very infrequency and the fact that a shooter can enjoy his sport for forty years and never witness so much as an accidental discharge, breed a dreaded complacency which itself can be the cause of a tragedy.

Make no mistake, any shotgun, from the humble .410 upwards, is a deadly weapon at close range. A blast from it can decapitate, eviscerate or remove a limb from the man standing next to you. To have that on your conscience must be an intolerable burden, but to remember that such an accident can happen in a split second is an important part of a shooting man's training. A conventional shotgun closed as opposed to broken (open) must be treated as loaded at all times. The three most dangerous things on a farm are a safe bull, a well-mended ladder and an unloaded gun: one mistake in the case of any of them could cost a life.

From our earlier examination of the mechanism of the shotgun, we know that the springs are permanently compressed with the sole exception of the time just after a shot, prior to the gun being opened: the breaking of a gun automatically cocks it. Thus, at all times, the hammers are poised ready to fall onto the firing pins and detonate a cartridge. That deceptive little word 'safe' which appears near the safety catch, is a snare for the unwary: all it means is that a sliver of metal prevents the triggers from being pulled. Metal and mechanical devices are as subject to malfunction as any man-made gadget, and a loaded gun leaned against a wall and knocked over by a dog, or dropped onto a hard surface or even given a sharp blow with the palm, is liable to go off, and who knows where the barrels may happen to be pointing in that fraught moment?

The rule is to treat every gun as though it were loaded and might go off at any minute. There are those who, when gently remonstrated with for careless gun handling, often reply breezily, 'It's all right, it's not loaded.' All I can add to that is, 'famous last words'. That man is allowed only one mistake. Quite simply, a gun should never be pointed at or near anyone else. If that rule were obeyed by all shooters, every accident would cease as of this moment.

It should become second nature that every time you pick up a gun or have one passed to you by someone else, you automatically

Don't stand next to this chap!

open it to ensure that it is not loaded. The other party will not take this as a slur on his own standards of safety, a good shooting man will expect you to do it and be surprised if you do not. These are the lethal moments: when you are clambering into a vehicle, deep in conversation as you struggle through a gap in the hedge, hopping about with the seat of your breeks caught on the barbed wire, hunting in the bushes for a lost bird or trying to slip a lead over the head of a recalcitrant dog. Just when you are distracted is the moment when the barrels swing wildly, passing the feet, midriffs or heads of goodness knows how many bystanders.

When out shooting, there are only two safe ways of carrying a gun: one is with muzzles pointing at the sky, the other with them pointing straight at the ground. Carry the weapon either in the crook of the arm with barrels down, or over the shoulder *with the trigger guard uppermost*. When expecting a shot, carry the gun at high port, resting the stock on your hip. At no time, except when firing, should your finger touch the trigger. Clay shooters and some continental sportsmen carry the gun broken, held by the muzzles with the stock over the shoulder. This looks sloppy and, in my opinion, is inappropriate for the shooting field.

When out shooting, you will often find it necessary to cross obstacles such as fences, boggy places, dense bushes or badly broken ground. A trip or a stumble in such a place could well cause an accidental discharge, so the rule is to break the gun and remove the cartridges when you come to such a hazard. Better to be safe than sorry and one accident is one too many. Carrying the gun broken and obviously empty is standard practice between drives when in company. Break it and pass it to a colleague when negotiating any especially awkward place. When you are alone, you have only yourself to think of, so the gun need not be carried broken. It is still important that no short cuts are taken on the general safety rules and the gun must still be unloaded when crossing a fence. Many a self-inflicted wound has been dealt by lone fowlers struggling through hedges, dragging the gun behind them. The lone gunner must be especially vigilant at checking that his barrels are clear before he loads. The smallest blockage of mud, sand or even snow is enough to bulge or burst the barrels. Regular glances up the barrel before loading is a good habit for any sort of field shooting. It is surprising how quickly it becomes automatic.

So much for the critical times between actually shooting the gun, but there are strict rules about that also. It is easy, in the heat of an exciting moment, to fire a dangerous shot. A highly prized quarry species such as a woodcock which flickers temptingly in front, sliding between the boles of the ash trees or darting through a gap in the firs, is often our undoing. Shoot now, quickly, or it will escape, the only woodcock I have seen all season! The rapid swing and shot are made with the positions of other guns, spectators or helpers far from your mind. One pellet of no.7 shot at 70 yards will blind a man who was innocently standing behind the firs.

'Never shoot where you can't see' was the old adage, and odd though it may sound, many a gaitered leg has been mistaken for a rabbit or dark shooting suit for a deer. 'Rabbit forward!' is the cry; you are ready, there is a rustle of something moving in the ferns in front of you, you see a flash of brown, your mind puts two and two together and you fire. Then it is too late; a beloved dog or a little boy could be dead as a result of your impetuosity. No shooter ever lost out through taking his time, through taking just one second to deliberate and assure himself that all is as it should be before he fires. Ask any beater how often in his life he has heard the shot whipping through the fronds above his head and you will appreciate how many otherwise safe shots make such mistakes. Shot falling to earth which patters down on the leaves is completely spent and totally harmless, so do not confuse it with shot still travelling straight from the barrel. Remember that what goes up, must come down.

The mistake which I believe is most commonly made, is shooting down the line. Even the oldest hands commit this crime and too often nobody seems to notice or take any action; potentially this is highly dangerous. Most commonly seen on driven shoots, but possible in any situation where the gun is not alone, shooting down the line means firing or aiming your gun which is in line with a neighbour. What happens is that a bird approaches in front; you pick it up with your muzzles as it approaches; its flight line takes it between you and the gun standing next to you. For some reason you delay firing, or you fire and miss with one barrel, and follow the bird as it passes in line with the next gun. It is easily done unless you are fully alive to the situation. The proper way is to engage in what action in front that you can, dismount the gun as the bird approaches the line, and remount when the bird has safely passed behind. Some shooting butts for notoriously low-flying birds such as grouse or partridge, have two long sticks, one on each side, which physically prevent the gun from being swung through at a dangerous angle. It is a most unnerving experience to follow comfortably through a perfectly safe passing covey, only to find that, a second later, you are pointing a loaded gun, safety catch off and your finger on the trigger, straight at the head of your brother.

Finally, just in case, make sure you are fully insured against personal accident and for third party. Membership of the British Association for Shooting and Conservation includes the premiums on a good policy. Shooting is a sport which involves guns, excitement, rough country, flowing adrenalin and, often, numbers of bystanders. To take out insurance for such a volatile activity is no more than common sense. With the best safety precautions in the world, gun accidents may be reduced but never eliminated.

Guns and small children are a deadly combination. Any shooter who leaves a gun or ammunition where a child may find it, is guilty of gross irresponsibility and has no right, in my view, to own a gun.

The points I made in the second chapter about pump action and semi-automatic shotguns should assume more relevance after having read the foregoing. A fellow sportsman may not, at a glance, see that such a gun is unloaded, so how do you pass it to him prior to crossing a fence? I have seen an 'empty' semi-automatic have its bolt operated vigorously six times to demonstrate that it was completely empty. It was snapped shut, the trigger pulled, and a ragged hole appeared in the kitchen wall. Never mind how it happened; enough to say that it did, and it is a fact of purest chance that the ragged hole did not appear in the middle of one of the five bystanders.

My final point on this vital matter is an important one, but many people find it difficult. What do you do if you see dangerous conduct by a fellow-gun? He may be older than you, more experienced, a well-established member of the shoot where you are a guest or maybe a close friend. When you are older, I think the answer is to speak up firmly, politely and directly to the culprit the moment the incident happens. If you are a novice in the shooting field, mention it to your father or your host, but do it

"Never shoot where you can't see."

quietly. If your host himself is responsible, do not go to that shoot again. Strong words? Indeed they are. Life is too precious to be risked because of our natural reluctance to make a 'scene'. I should hate to think of my lifeless carcase being carried home on a hurdle to my widow and orphans with the only epitaph, 'He was too polite to complain.' Speak up every time. Some will take your comments gratefully, others may be aggressive but do not worry; both will think of what you have said, and only by such happenings can anyone be expected to improve. Have the difficult conversation in private and not in front of others. If you are not asked again, then so be it. Only an unsporting host would be so unkind, so you are better off out of it.

Finally, remember at all times Sir Mark Beaufoy's final couplet, 'All the pheasants ever bred, won't repay for one man dead'.

SHOOTING STRAIGHT

These notes are written for the majority of shooters who shoot from the right shoulder. If you are one of those who, like me, shoots from the left shoulder, then for 'right' read 'left' and vice versa throughout. The left hand holds the gun at the fore-end but no finger or thumb should curl over the top of the barrels. The right hand grasps the small of the butt with the trigger finger on the edge of the trigger guard. The right hand should be under the gun so that the elbow does not come up when the gun is raised to the shoulder: this will encourage the good habit of lifting the gun rather than pushing it forwards. The thumb should be round the stock and not left on top in line with the top lever as this can result in a nasty bruise or the accidental pushing forward of the safety catch after the first shot. The grip should be firm and be far enough back so that the ball of the trigger finger reaches the front trigger. Do not pull the trigger with the knuckle part of the finger: this makes you slow at changing triggers and pushes the right hand hard against the back of the trigger guard which may cause cutting or bruising as a result of the recoil.

The hands should be on the gun in this way when a shot is expected at any moment. At the same time, hold the gun with the stock tucked under the right forearm, so that the barrels have the shortest distance to travel before they are on target. Good gun mounting is most of the art of good shooting. Master it and you are on the way to becoming a good shot. Like many other skills, it is a purely physical knack, a co-ordination of hand and eye like hitting a cricket ball or bouncing on a trampoline. Some will have a greater natural aptitude for it than others, and those who are so

Remember, a neighbour may be up on a bank or hidden by a fold in the ground.

physically unco-ordinated that they are total failures, are very few indeed.

Fix your eye firmly on the target, concentrating on its head. Your internal computer will assess its speed and line of flight and in a single, fluid movement, raise the gun to the target. It should feel as though, with both arms, you are pushing your gun forward towards the bird; this is done with the eye unwaveringly on the bird and *not* on the barrels of the gun. The beginner is over-concerned with the heel of the stock and bedding it in the shoulder, but it is much more important to put the end of the barrel at the bird. The other common mistake is to put the gun to the shoulder, irrespective of the disposition of the target and only then begin to aim it, like a rifle. This leads to a fault known as poking and hence the inevitable miss. If you can point the gun at the bird as easily and with the same movement as you would point your left index finger, then you have the ability to shoot and kill.

The problem of lead is one which perplexes the novice, but I believe we concern ourselves with it too much. It is quite clear that if a stationary gun is pointed at a flying bird, the time it takes for the brain to say 'Pull', the muscles to respond, the cartridge to detonate and the shot arrive at the right place is also time enough for the target to have travelled several feet, or, the further off and faster it is, yards.

To reduce this problem, recall what I have written about gun mounting. If you have done it properly and put the muzzles to the speeding bird, they will already be moving with it. What you do next is one of the hardest things to put into words; many have tried, and the number of poor shots still to be found, are a bad advertisement for the power of the written or spoken word when translated into actions. My theory (and practice) is to swing with the bird, overtake it by a distance I believe to be commensurate with its speed, *keep swinging* and tap the trigger a crisp blow with the ball of the finger. In my case and, I suspect, the cases of others, misses are caused mainly by a failure to judge the speed of the bird, its range and its angle of flight. For example, a pheasant flushed from a hedge bottom and blundering away, appears to be flying parallel to the ground, but in fact it is rising at quite a sharp angle. A failure to judge this correctly leads to birds missed below and behind.

'If your eye is on the bird and you are mounting correctly, you haven't got to worry about anything at all' – thus wrote that classic shooting coach Robert Churchill. I make no apology for repeating the dictum. It applies to a bird coming towards you, going away or crossing. The fast-approaching bird in front, such as a speeding grouse or partridge, used to be a terror for me, until an old farmer told me to 'blot it out with the barrels, lad: if you can see it when you shoot, you've missed it.' I immediately put the advice into practice and now that bird is my favourite target. All the old farmer was doing was using his own form of words to explain exactly what I have been saying rather more long-windedly. It makes sense, for as the partridge is coming into range, your gun muzzles pick it out, move with it, overtake it until they conceal it, the stock touches the shoulder and bang! one dead partridge.

By the same token, the going-away, rising bird must be approached in the same way with the same result, we hope; if we can see it when we shoot, we are under it. A bird coming from behind or a pigeon dropping to decoys calls for the opposite treatment: if it is dropping and you blot it out, you will miss behind; you must be able to see it above your smoothly swinging barrels.

Much of shooting style is a matter of instinct, and like the business of ballistics on which I touched in an earlier chapter, it can do more harm than good to become obsessed with all the technical arguments. Some brilliant shots have never had a shooting lesson in their lives and give the matter of lead, swing and forward allowance not a thought.

If we accept that much of the skill is instinctive and only a little of it learned, there is little we can do by the way of 'dry' practice. Even so, there is much that may be done in the living room at home by standing in the 'ready' position mounting the gun and 'firing' at various objects such as door knobs, light shades or pictures. Mount and swing along the pelmet or picture rail; by varying your position in the room, you can simulate every angle of flight line. Practise saying 'bang' at the moment you would have fired. Do not pull the trigger of an unloaded or empty gun, and certainly do not allow the hammers to fall on empty chambers, or serious damage to the gun will result. If you feel unable to achieve realism by saying 'bang', snap caps should be used. They will take the blow of the firing pin without damage, and will allow the ejectors to work properly.

Another important aspect of good shooting is footwork. Many physical activities depend for their success on the feet being in the right place at the right time. Some books go into great detail and show diagrams of patterns of feet moving about like the old-fashioned instruction manuals on ballroom dancing. The simple rule is weight on the left (forward) foot – never be caught flat footed with weight on both, or a wild shot and a miss are inevitable. As I have mentioned earlier, time spent standing behind a gun on a game or clay shoot is never wasted. When watching an expert, do not bother to watch the target, a common mistake, for it will fall almost every time. Watch the style of the shooter; analyse his mount, swing and footwork. A good man, as in any sport, will make it look unhurried and easy. Try to absorb some of what you see into your own shooting. You may find yourself able actually to see the shot column as it whizzes through the air; this is not as ridiculous as it may sound since experienced clay coaches can see it all the time, a grey, elongated smudge flashing towards the target.

It is important to appreciate the limitations of your gun. It is most effective at close range and after that, the all-important pattern begins to deteriorate. Hence your judgement of range is vital. The secret here is to assess distance by associating it with a measurement which is easy to identify. How high are those poplars, and is the bird higher or lower? Is this bird more or less than a cricket pitch away? Is this shot roughly the length of the garden at home? – and so on. The trick is harder in a featureless landscape such as a saltmarsh or an open moor, but the knack comes with experience. You will learn that various quarry species present certain identifying features which let you know it is in range.

Gun pointing directly at the next man – not popular.

CLAY PIGEON SHOOTING

I wrote earlier, in passing, that the clay bird has become a sport in its own right and at top level, a highly competitive one at that. This is not a book for the clay buster, but the clay bird can be made to simulate many of the targets you are likely to meet in the field, so it is no bad idea to join a clay-pigeon club; the sport is so popular that there is bound to be one in your area. Most clubs are affiliated to the Clay Pigeon Shooting Association (CPSA) and operate within its rules. As well as the actual shooting, membership of a clay club will accustom you to mixing with crowds of people of whom many have guns. Clay shoot safety rules are, if anything, more strictly enforced than those in the field. Should you wave your unbroken gun around in a dangerous manner, your fellow-guns or the officials will show none of the diffidence of pheasant shooters, but will tell you shortly and crisply exactly what you have done wrong, and not to do it again.

Clay shooting offers a variety of stereotyped shots, which practitioners of the sport are pleased to call 'disciplines'. Down the line is a bird released from in front of you and flying low and fast away from you. Once you have the knack, it is possible to get every one: experts can. The bird is addressed usually from five points in a shallow arc behind the trap: the gun stands at each point in turn.

Most fun for the sporting field shooter is what is known as English Sporting. Types of target can be roughly divided into four groups. The going away, the incomer, the right-to-left crosser and the left-to-right crosser. Master these four, and you will find that the skills suit most sporting targets which are really only variations on the basic four. The going away places a premium on good gun mounting – an error at twenty yards becomes progressively greater at forty yards. Two diverging lines of target and pellets can never meet. Once the straightaway bird is mastered, the shooter can vary the degree of elevation and move his angle to right and left.

The incoming target can be high or low and angled from right or left, but representing perfectly the driven bird. A pheasant or partridge is usually accelerating when you come to shoot at it. Stand too far back for an incoming clay and it will seem to decelerate, until it seems almost to hover before falling to earth. Stand back until you get the hang of the shot, moving closer to the trap as your performance improves. The nearer to the trap you stand, the faster the bird and the less time you have to address it. Incomers thrown at you too low are as potentially dangerous as a low bird in the field so beware of them. In addition, a low-flying clay is a dangerous missile which can deliver a grievous wound, while shattered fragments spinning down are more than potent

Dangerous gun carrying.

enough to blind the gun or a bystander. Many clay shooters wear spectacles for that very reason.

For the two crossing birds, from right to left and vice versa, it is best to start with the bird at right angles which is the easier, and then begin to vary the angle, your distance from the target and the point at which you fire at it. This bird will expose problems of the wrong master eye which causes missing in front or behind; in front for the right to left, and behind for the left to right.

Once you become reasonably proficient, birds may be presented to you as doubles, either both at once or the second 'on report' or released when you fire at the first. For crossing birds fire at the near target first and let the gun swing smoothly without check to take the leading bird with your second barrel.

If you cannot, for any reason, join a CPSA club, there are other options open to you. Many country fairs nowadays run little clay shoots, and while this is not the time to practise, at least you have the opportunity to try your hand at a variety of birds without worrying too much about your score. Better still are those fairs such as the Country Landowners' Association Game Fair or the many fairs where the coaching clinics of the BASC are featured. For a modest fee an expert will give you instruction on a particular bird and help you to identify where you are going wrong.

There are shooting schools with properly qualified coaches specializing in instructing anyone from the raw novice to the expert who needs a little revision before the season opens. This is the best training possible with high-quality instruction and the latest gadgetry in traps, high towers and other facilities. The trouble is that lessons are expensive and so need to be strictly rationed. If you are lucky enough to have a lesson at such a school, perhaps thanks to an indulgent uncle or parent, take full advantage of the occasion, remember what you have been told and try to put it into practice when on your own. A good coach can diagnose faults and correct them. The younger you are, the less ingrained your faults will be and so putting them right is easier than for an older man.

A common arrangement is for a group of friends to form their own clay shoot on an informal basis. For this a suitable piece of ground must be found, a trap or traps obtained, a fund started to provide targets, full authority from the landowner received and absolute standards of safety and organization insisted upon. 'Casual' may be the spirit of the affair, but there can be nothing casual about safety.

Our little game shoot runs such a clay group. We have two second-hand traps and use our imagination to turn a derelict barn, a pile of straw bales, some mounds of earth and an abandoned water tower into sites for showing a variety of birds. Protection for the trapper is essential, for one stray pellet is enough to blind him, so he must have something really substantial between himself and the guns. Half a sheet of rusty corrugated iron is not good enough. It is easy enough to organize and there is none of the pressure of competition which is attendant on more formal clay shooting. By the same token, all you need for practice is a trap, a trapper, a clay and yourself, suitably armed. Cheap, portable traps (such as the Bowman with its own sledge stand) which fit into the boot of a car are ideal for the purpose. Again, make sure that you shoot in a safe place, away from stock, vulnerable farm crops and buildings and that you have the full permission of the farmer. Remember that you may not fire your gun, or have it loaded, in a public place, so do not attempt to practise in the local municipal park!

The cream of clay shooting for the field shooter must be FITASC. This discipline sets out to imitate real shooting situations by presenting a variety of sporting shots in a realistic setting. Bolting rabbits whizz unexpectedly from behind bushes, crows float over the ash poles, woodcock flicker through the firs, high pheasants stream overhead while pairs of grouse curl over the brow. This, for me, is the cream of clay shooting, and while I have not had the pleasure of doing it often enough, it is the only clay shooting about which I feel myself becoming animated.

The clay bird is a good trainer for the pure physical skills of shooting, but field shooting is about much more. It calls for field craft and gives a buzz of adrenalin. A missed pheasant is cause for more concern than a missed clay. One goose in the bag is a greater triumph than hitting fifty 'straight' down-the-line clays.

For those who wish to make a study of English and American skeet, Olympic trap or trench, Automatic Ball trap, and the other specialities, this is not the book for you; *A Manual of Clayshooting* by Chris Cradock (Batsford), on the other hand, definitely is.

Low shots can be dangerous to the beaters.

8
The Quarry

This is not, nor does it set out to be an exhaustive list. We will look at a cross-section of sporting birds of the types the all-round shooter might be likely to encounter. A shooting man must have a wider knowledge of his quarry than just the manner in which it flies over his head. He must understand its distribution, favourite habitat, nesting and breeding habits and so much about it that he can come to think like a pheasant, wigeon or whatever.

The Pheasant is so widely distributed and familiar to everyone that it needs little introduction. It is the commonest and most conspicuous sporting bird and probably the most popular, an opinion which the grouse man or partridge purist might dispute. The pheasant is not a native bird, and popular opinion is that it came originally from China and was introduced in Britain as a table bird by the Romans. There is a Romano–British mosaic in existence which depicts a fine, ring-necked cock pheasant. The bird is easily reared, tough, adaptable to changes in farming practice and hardy. It is likely today that very few pheasants are more than two generations removed from reared stock.

The modern pheasant owes some of its resilience to the fact that it is a descendant of mixed race. There are several strains from the

Cock pheasant, stone dead and falling.

almost black melanistic to the traditional ring neck, the metallic green Japanese, the almost buff Bohemian and others. The strains interbreed freely so that pheasants showing the features of more than one type are common.

The pheasant has rightly been described as a bird of the borders because of its love of the edges of woods, the fringes of hedge bottoms and the outskirts of marshes. It is found everywhere in the British Isles except in north-west Scotland and the South Wales coast. Its favourite ground is cultivated land or pasture with woodland or some cover nearby. It is also fond of marshes with reed beds or parkland but less fond of open moorland, although a pheasant may be flushed from virtually anywhere. It likes to roost in hawthorn bushes, firs and low trees, but in open country such as the Fens, it will roost or 'jug' on the ground or on a dyke bank. The pheasant is an uncomplicated and bold eater, eating weed seeds, corn, leaves, fruit, small insects, garden plants and acorns.

It nests in thick cover such as beds of nettles, brambles or cow parsley from early April onwards. One cock will service a number of hens, defending his harem and his territory against rival cocks. A hen pheasant may lay up to sixteen eggs, and it is not unknown for them to lay eggs in one another's nests. Eggs and young are easily predated by crows, foxes, feral cats, stoats, mink, hedgehogs and weasels; they are also lost to prolonged spells of cold wet weather just after hatching time, which is generally in the three-week period from the middle of May to 8 June.

Modern gamekeepers find it more convenient to rear large numbers of birds than to check and protect a series of nests scattered about the shoot. Reared birds are released in woods or suitable cover, and fed and protected there until they have acclimatized to outdoor life and have learned the local geography. Reared pheasants are notorious strayers and walk away from the shoot, a field a day, until many of them have found their way to a neighbour's ground. Rearing is not cheap, and each lost bird means lost money, so the preservation of a suitable and quiet habitat, easy availability of food and no predators plus daily 'dogging in', or walking potential strayers back home, are some of the methods of reducing straying. Some old keepers make up a secret potion, the composition of which is known only to themselves, which they mix with the food. To date, no one has proved that any of it works. As for predation, a fox breaking into a release pen will wantonly kill a hundred pheasants in a night, so the importance of protection against such losses is an important matter.

A keeper will gradually feed his birds away from the rearing

Two cocks skim out over the guns – rather low but by no means easy. Note muzzles safely up.

wood to another piece of cover some distance away. On a shooting day he will drive this cover in the direction of 'home', and the pheasants will need little urging to fly in that direction as quickly as they can, and so provide hard shots. The idea of organized game shooting is to provide targets which test the guns, so shoots with valleys will drive the birds from hilltop to hilltop, and the most famous shoots are those which can do just that.

The pheasant may be shot in many ways and in different circumstances. A walked-up bird flushed from an overgrown ditch can be exciting, especially if it comes of some good dog work, a little fieldcraft and a minor plan of campaign. Like most game birds, the pheasant is attractive to dogs, and a dog is essential for rough shooting. A wounded pheasant will run for half a mile and, like as not, go to ground down a rabbit hole. It is far beyond the capability of a human being to recover such a bird in overgrown country and it must be left to die miserably. A dog of even moderate ability and training will recover such a bird.

For the novice shooter weaned on pigeons and rabbits, the pheasant is likely to be the first game bird he shoots. Its handsome appearance and excellence on the table make it a trophy of which to be proud. On some high-powered shoots, there has been a trend towards shooting what I believe to be unwarrantable bags of birds, often running into many hundreds in a day. In shooting, More does not necessarily mean Beautiful. A brace of birds fairly hunted, flushed, shot and retrieved is worth a great number of poor-quality reared ones pushed out of a wood and over your head.

Even so, potentially the driven pheasant offers the best target. Classic game shots, familiar with all game birds over many years, put the high, curling pheasant, planing on set wings at extreme range as top of their list of difficult shots. An old cock grouse hugging the contours of the moor and jinking at top speed over the butts will run it a close second.

Rearing a few pheasants at home to improve the stock of any ground where you have permission to shoot, is a comparatively simple matter. Eggs may be bought or collected from nests on ground where you have permission to do so. Quite often a farm worker will save a nest from the mower. Small, domestic incubators with about one hundred-egg capacity may be bought and a paraffin brooder. A small, wire run and a patch of fresh grass and a bag of feed (high protein), pellets are all you require. Nothing will give you a better insight into the ways of any creature than rearing it from birth to maturity. Whatever grouse and partridge men may claim, the pheasant is the bedrock on which most British field shooting and allied trades and industries is built.

One of the real pleasures of a day's driven pheasant shooting is that period when you are at your peg waiting for things to happen. It can be quite a long wait. Unseen by you, distant beaters will be blanking-in stubbles, tapping along hedgerows and bringing in far-off spinneys. On a shoot with which you are unfamiliar, you might well imagine that you have been forgotten and that the beaters were driving towards a row of untenanted pegs on another part of the shoot. It was just so with me one day in January when guns lined an exposed Suffolk field of heavy clay, wet underfoot, while a biting nor'easter drove stinging snow pellets parallel to the ground. There was no sight nor sound of a beater for a good forty minutes while we stood there, a row of chilly monoliths on a Neaderthal hillside. That the action, when it came, was as hot as the weather was cold, is incidental. The best part of fifty pheasants in ten minutes did much to restore the circulation to fingertips and noses.

Preferable are those waits when the weather is benign; when the sun shines from a cloudless sky; when there is a touch of frost on old stubbles and a healthy tang in the air. There is much to see as you stand musing in front of your own particular patch of quiet woodland. I recall another day, also in Suffolk, when I found myself in front of a remnant of the primeval forest which once clothed most of the southern counties. Massive trees reared above a criss-cross maze of fallen timber and impenetrable thicket which must have provided sanctuary for outlaws and wolves alike. The great forest was, by the ancients, correctly deemed an effective barrier to the waves of invaders which swept the country. Hence, Roman, Saxon and Norman tended to travel on the open chalk downlands where only grass grew and the going was easy. Because of this, the earthworks thrown up by retreating locals usually span the chalklands. In that way, the invader was faced with the bristling stakes and armed warriors on the dyke, the fenny swamps at one end, and the impenetrable oak forests at the other.

It was one of the few remaining scraps of this wood at which I now gazed. True, it had been tidied up a bit since the days of Uther Pendragon, but there was still good harbourage for pheasants and even roe deer, four of which bounded gracefully out across the winter corn as we approached. The tangle of fallen trunks had gone, but the great oaks had resisted passing centuries and there were plenty of brambles. The oaks were leafless and crabby, massive and knobbly of bole with intriguing holes here and there which looked custom made for owls, stockdoves and jack-daws. The bark was crusty and crannied and it provided shelter for multitudes of insects and cocoons. As I looked, a treecreeper slid, mouselike, along one gnarled limb, the delicate forceps of its beak searching every nook for food. It fluttered a few feet to the next branch and continued the hunt, dodging round and up. It was followed by a family of long-tailed tits, at least a dozen of them, flying in a string like a shower of blown thistledown and, like the

A covey breaks over a thorn hedge.

treecreeper, minutely examining the cracks and crevices for – what else but titbits? It is surprising that after such regular and meticulous searchings of their hiding places any insect lives long enough to see the spring. The long-tailed tits doubtless had their bottle-shaped, lichenous nest somewhere nearby, into which the whole flock would huddle for warmth at night, emerging next morning, one at a time, like a well-executed conjuring trick.

From further down the wood came the harsh rattle of a jay; they love oaks for the same reason as pheasants – acorns. 'Jay!' called someone, in case we had not noticed. The bird had seen a distant beater toiling, antlike, down the far slope and was crying a warning. He was too crafty to come over guns standing in the open, and I caught sight of the flash of his white rump as he flicked away along the boundary hedge where, needless to say, no one was standing.

The deer had, as I mentioned, fled the wood at our approach. Deer are, of course, never shot on pheasant drives on this shoot, but they had learned during the season, and realized that soon beaters would be coming to rouse them from their couches and so they opted for an early and dignified departure. They even took the time to stop and give us a long, hard stare, before they tripped daintily over the skyline. It was easy to see why the roe liked that particular piece of woodland. There were plenty of brambles for them to eat, some dense thickets in which they could hide, a good mixture of timber of all ages and a retreat which was remote and little disturbed. Were these beasts, I mused, descendants of the roe which haunted the great forests in the time of Athelstan and which formed the natural prey of wolves? It was a happy thought, and it just might have been true. The keeper had said that there was also a large badger sett in the middle of the wood. The inhabitants rarely touched the gamebirds and Brock was left to himself. Badgers, too, might have lived thereabouts for centuries. Although I never saw him, my nose told me that a fox had been that way during the morning, for a whiff of his pungent reek was suddenly carried to me by an eddy in the breeze. While the numbers on this shoot are controlled by the keepers, they are not shot on shooting days. Even the keepers themselves admit to not wanting to exterminate the last one – which is as it should be. An estate without a fox is a poor sort of place.

A distant whistle shrilled to show that the final phase of the drive was about to begin. A cloud of pigeon rising from the distant ash poles showed to a yard where the line was forming. Then there came the sound of a faint, woody tapping, a sinister, muffled rattle of sticks on tree trunks, not loud but a far more effective mover of pheasants than any amount of stentorian bellowing. A tawny owl came floating and flapping from where he had been disturbed from his roost in the firs. Bemused by the daylight he drifted past us, over the field, and into the next spinney, there to resume his interrupted slumbers. Then it was blackbirds with their chip-chipping alarm notes, dashing round the bushes and back the way they had come. A shower of finches, twittering feebly, were busying themselves in the topmost twigs; a grey squirrel caught the eye as he tried to make up his mind which side of the tree-trunk was the safest against which to flatten himself. The whole wood was a mass of tiny movements.

A cock pheasant ran to the edge of the wood, looked out at us, crouched to spring, thought better of it, and darted back into the covert, his feet rustling audibly in the dry leaves. Others came, looked, and went, criss-crossing each other's tracks in the open spaces, each one sure that it alone knew the best escape route.

As the sticks came nearer, the pheasants began to mass inside the edge of the wood. Guns were on their toes; the long period of waiting and gradual build-up of excitement had reached a fine pitch. Thumbs felt to make sure safety catches were still there; feet shuffled to stamp down the already level ground. This was the critical time in the drive when the keeper did not want his birds to flush in one great cloud, but preferred to flush them in small numbers. A rash boy or a wild dog can spoil everything. This man knew his job. Four birds, bolder than the rest, ran out to the bleached grass on the brim of the boundary dyke. They crouched, bunched their leg muscles and sprang aloft.

With a harsh whirring of wings and throaty chuckling, the first cock of the day came rocketing towards me.

The Partridge

The story of the *partridge* is an interesting one. There are two distinct species, the English or grey partridge and the French or red-legged partridge. There have been attempts to rear and release first crosses between the red-leg and the chukor, a bird named the ogridge, but the value of the experiment is far from proven. Most shooting men have a soft spot for the grey partridge, partly because it is a true native of the British Isles and partly because it is as interesting a bird to shoot as it is good on the table.

The Grey Partridge was the common game bird of the lowland farms in Edwardian and Victorian England. A fairly haphazard farming system which left rioting hedges, weed-ridden fields, unchecked hordes of insects and a mixed pattern of roots and cereals suited it perfectly. The chicks fed exclusively on insects (mainly sawfly larvae) for the first few days of their lives and of them there was no shortage. Wide dyke banks made perfect nesting sites, the turnip fields gave shelter, and long, unkempt stubbles left well into the winter before they were ploughed provided the perfect habitat during the late months. Then the partridge was king, and some huge bags, sometimes running to a thousand or more in a day, were shot on the famous partridge manors at places like Six Mile Bottom, Holkham and Elveden.

The last fifty years have seen a sad decline. Farming is now highly efficient and commercial. Fields are huge, hedges are uprooted at the rate of hundreds of miles a year, cropping is intensive and weeds and insects are rigorously controlled. The plough is in the field almost as soon as the combine has left and the stubble been burned off. The grey partridge has no food, no nesting cover and none of the patchwork quilt of mixed farming which it loves. Its numbers have dwindled sadly and at times in the last few years, its very survival has been in jeopardy. Gone are the coveys pouring out of the autumn turnips in bewildering numbers; gone are the 150-brace days of grandfather's time. To shoot just one brace today on a mixed shooting day is a matter for comment and also slight regret that there are now two less of them. The Game Conservancy has widely researched the life of the grey partridge and there is little left to find out about it. It makes recommendations to farmers who wish to increase partridge stocks and it can be done with little or no interference to farm practice.

The grey partridge is a small round gamebird with generally olive brown, delicately striped plumage. Both sexes are similar and have an orange-chestnut face, chestnut flanks and tail and a striking brown horseshoe on the lower breast. The cry is a rusty creaking like an unoiled hinge, a sound once common in the evenings on any lowground farm in the country. It favours mixed farmland with rough grass, woodland and open ground and is very fond of sandy heaths and marshland but less so of high moorland. It spends little time on the wing, preferring to crouch or run from its enemies. Family groups are known as coveys and they tend to stay together until breeding season, roosting in a circle on the ground, each bird facing outwards, the better to see approaching danger. Partridges are monogamous and pair for life. They nest on the ground at the bottom of hedges or in rough grassland and, like any ground-nesting gamebird, their nests are easily predated; chicks can be quickly lost in their first few critical days of life. Peak hatching time coincides with Royal Ascot week, and a few days of storms at that time will effectively put paid to the partridge shooting for the season.

Shooting driven grey partridges is considered by many to be the cream of the sport. The bird has good staying power, and the same birds may be shown to the guns several times in the same day. For driving, the guns stand behind a line of butts or a tall hawthorn hedge. The birds are driven in with great skill, for showing partridges is a real but vanishing art. It involves a gentle approach, moving the wary birds into cover without causing them to panic and fly off explosively in all directions. Beaters on the flanks will be carrying white flags, the better to keep the covey moving quietly on the right line. The beaters slowly advance and then the birds flush, not in one great flock but a covey at a time, led by an old cock bird, which flies forward towards the distant hedge. Let the leader so much as suspect that danger lurks and he will lead his party safely out over a flank. In this respect it is vital that the guns maintain absolute silence. As the birds cross the hedge, they see the guns and the covey explodes like a star shell, each bird flaring and banking to escape. This is partridge shooting at its best and it calls for a high degree of skill to drop a right and left out of them.

Even if the keeper blows his whistle to signal the approach of a covey, the gun has only a few seconds to pick his target, instinctively swing and shoot and change to another. The old masters with double guns could take two in front and two behind with a skill only rarely seen today. A covey of eight once flew between Lord Walsingham and his equally adept neighbour, Lord Ripon, both shooting two guns. Each gun took a right and left from them and thus, effectively, bagged the lot. The point of the story is less to demonstrate the high degree of shooting skill but more to highlight the expertise shown by each gun in picking out his own four birds.

The old method was to walk-up partridges over setters and pointers or even a kite, shaped like a hawk and operated by a boy, which had the effect of making the covey squat and therefore more easy to approach. Mainly for this reason were guns bored with the more open barrel firing first. The open pattern took a bird as it rose, and the more tightly choked, second barrel took the next when it was further away. The reverse borings are more suitable for driven game, and despite the fact that driving is now more practised than walking-up, game guns are still bored in the old, traditional way.

Walking-up partridges is now out of favour. Time was when on 1 September, the opening day of the season, every sportsman was out tramping the stubbles. The shots were not especially challenging, big bags of a diminishing species might be made, and the slowest and latest birds to rise were the ones which tended to be shot. These were the very birds which should be preserved and the old ones shot. On a driven shoot, the leading bird is the one the gun addresses first and that is the old-timer. Walking-up grey partridges is not a good idea.

The French or Red-legged partridge was introduced during this century as a supplement to the stocks of indigenous greys. Similar in size and shape to the grey partridge, the red-leg is far more colourful, both sexes having a white eye stripe, throat and cheeks with a handsome black border. The flanks are very distinctive with blue, chestnut and white bars. The rest of the plumage is grey and olive brown with handsome rufous tail feathers. The beak and legs are sealing-wax red.

Its distribution is less general than that of the grey, being found in the Midlands and Eastern counties, but hardly at all in Scotland and the extreme west of the country. Its favourite haunts also are similar to grey partridge country, with mixed or arable low-ground farms being favourite. It too nests on the ground in rough corners, and a cock will hold a territory against intruders. As a sporting proposition, the red-leg turned out to be a mixed blessing. It is certainly more hardy than the English bird and, although nests and young are easily predated, there tends to be a better survival rate. It is easy to rear and prolific and does not show the tendency to stray like a pheasant or the grey partridge; fifty poults released in a wood and properly fed and cared for, will stay within a field of the spot for the whole season, dispersing only in spring when the breeding urge comes upon them.

On the debit side, a red-leg prefers to use its legs rather than wings. It is a notorious runner and has been known to run between the standing guns or back between the dogs and beaters. On heavy ground their feet pick up mud and grow heavy; the birds may be picked up by hand or by dogs. When they do fly, they can manage one spectacular, explosive flight over a hedge, especially on a windy day, and can show good sport. That one effort is enough for them, and you are unlikely to see that covey on the wing again on the same day. Greater success has been achieved by treating red-legs like pheasants and releasing them in cover or woods instead of on more open, traditional partridge ground. In this situation they will flush singly or in small numbers and fly hard and fast over the guns. Often a Frenchman will fly low, quite often intending to pitch at the foot of the hedge behind which the gun is standing. Often too they will fly past a gun at head height and these two habits make them the unwitting cause of dangerous situations or accidents. A high proportion of accidental pepperings in the field are caused, if not by woodcock, then by low partridges.

The Red Grouse, to many shooters lucky enough to have the chance to pursue it, is considered the king of game birds. There are many curious things about it which intrigue us. It is found only

A grouse in the bag.

in the UK. Not only is it impossible to rear and release it for shooting but it is also a truly wild creature, an almost exclusive feeder, and if it cannot get its shoots of young heather, it will die. It lives in wild and cruel country, the heathery hill-tops of Yorkshire and Scotland where fierce gales, snowdrifts, cold rains, fogs and little or no shelter are the norm. The bird is subject to many internal parasites which sap its strength and eventually kill it. An overpopulation in a good breeding year will be followed the next by a thinning out caused by disease. It is hard to over shoot grouse, any cock bird left without its own feeding territory by Christmas will be chivvied from pillar to post by birds which have secured their own patch, and will surely be dead by the New Year.

The red grouse is rather larger than a partridge with longer wings and a strong, fast flight which follows the contours of a hill, but from time to time it will do a half-tumble sideways and jink, making it a hard bird to shoot. Its plumage is a rich reddish-brown speckled and barred with white and chocolate. The female is more heavily barred and slight duller in colour than the cock. The feet and legs are heavily feathered from autumn and through the winter; this is to prevent heat loss in an inhospitable climate. In summer the cock develops red wattles and becomes very aggressive, even attacking humans and dogs if they approach too near. It nests in the heather, but crows, hill foxes, harriers and hawks take a heavy toll of eggs and chicks. There is little a keeper can do to help the bird except control those predators which may legally be killed (all hawks are fully protected) and burn off the old heather in rotation so that there are always new shoots sprouting. Some old heather is left for shelter in hard weather. In really bad conditions, grouse come down from the high ground to the valley fields or up to the high tops above the snow.

Grouse hatch generally towards the middle to the end of June and bad weather in that month invariably means a bad season.

Grouse are shot in three ways. They can be walked-up, with a number of guns in line, interspersed with beaters and accompanied by dogs. They can be shot over pointers or setters. Here it would be normal for there to be only two guns walking along behind the dogs which range far and wide over the moor. The pointer scents the grouse and halts, and the guns then come up to the point, one on either side of the dog. This form of shooting is normally practised in the far north of Scotland, particularly Sutherland and Caithness. Lastly there is the driven grouse which for many is the cream of all shooting.

It is then that the coveys are driven by teams of well-drilled beaters, towards a line of butts strategically placed. A grouse butt is itself a work of art, being built of stones and turf, blending perfectly with the terrain and once placed, there for ever. The grouse will always fly in the same direction if driven a certain way, for there are none of the local, annual differences caused by cover crops being planted elsewhere, as on a lowground shoot.

To stand in a grouse butt on a fine autumn day is one of the real peaks of a shooting man's life and, sad to say, there are many keen shooters who will never experience that particular delight. The sun beams down and the air is heavy with the scent of heather in full bloom. The pattern of cloud and sunshine glides across the green, grey and purple hills. Rocky outcrops catch the eye, silver threads of streams run down the mountain side, sheep nibble and baa. Dragonflies and butterflies flicker over the heather. In the distance, a gutteral 'bec bec – go bec' shows that at least one old cock grouse is sitting up on a tussock and aware that something is up. For the gun, waiting quietly, his gun ready, his cartridges laid in ranks on the parapet of the butt, this is a time of great excitement and keen anticipation. Nerve ends are a tingle – even a bumble bee seen on the skyline has you fooled into thinking it is a grouse and has you on your toes.

Then, far away, you see a pinprick of white moving on the skyline. It is a flag held by a beater as he plods on, one of a straight line of twenty, steadily pushing the birds forward as they go. Then the moment arrives; there is the shrill of a distant whistle; a cluster of black specks appears far off in front – they are coming your way. Nearer and nearer they come, and you prepare to mount your gun at the leader, but find that you had hopelessly underestimated their pace, for with a whirr of wings, at incredible speed, they are on you, about your ears and before you can turn round to try a going-away shot, they are out of range behind.

When you finally get their measure and raise the gun to them at what seems an impossible range in front, blot one out, give a last-minute upward flick of the barrels to take account of their great speed and see the bird so fast and unhittable bouncing on the heather clumps and a pinch of pale feathers drifting, you can safely say that, as a shooting man, you have sampled the best. Walking-up may not offer quite such difficult shots; it is still exciting and no activity for the weak of limb or scant of breath. The grouse bursting unexpectedly in front of you, whirring off on clockwork wings with a sardonic, throaty chuckle are easy enough to miss. Because of its comparative scarcity and the demand for it by high-paying sportsmen, many of them from overseas, grouse shooting of any sort is an expensive sport. Landowners with thinly populated, unkeepered moorland will sometimes give permission to friends to have 'a walk round', but be prepared for hard work and light bags.

Big toe trouble – or perhaps I should say, trouble with the big toe, was almost enough to mar my personal 12 August. I feel that pulled muscles, creaking joints and aching bones are as nothing compared with sore feet – a sore foot even, nay, the smallest spot on one foot. The muscles often demand retribution the day after, but the immediate agony of a blister or rubbed heel demands instant acknowledgement. Mine started the day as no more than a hint of pressure on the nearside big toe where it came into contact with the inside of the boot. It was certainly not a thing about which to worry, but as the day wore on, that tiny spot of tightness wore into the consciousness, grew and then loomed until it dominated my whole existence.

Coming down a hill was worse than going up, for each downward step slid the weight forward, jamming the toe even more excruciatingly against the toe-cap. When I finally returned to base and eased off the offending boot, my foot seemed to heave an almost audible sigh of relief while the spot which had given me so much agony turned out to be a blister no bigger than a pea. The moral is an old one but it could do with repetition: wear unfamiliar boots for a few days before indulging in the prolonged route march which walking-up grouse involves. You may cause a certain amount of comment as you clump round the office in commando-soled hill boots, but it saves a good deal of anguish later.

Apart from big toe trouble, it was a good day to be out. We may chuckle at the stories of people pausing 'to admire the view' in order to snatch a quick breather and we can even bring to mind what it feels like to walk for an hour up a ling-clad slope of 1:4, but nothing is quite like the real thing. A moorland keeper once told me that hill walking was just a matter of putting one foot before the other: how undeniable but what a gross understatement, what a travesty of the real truth. A steep hill, walked once a year, is an excellent barometer of advancing age and a reminder that one may be approaching the time of life when care must be taken when indulging in unfamiliar exercise.

This 12 August was a day of hot sunshine and stiff wind. The moor was parched with drought, the usually knee-deep boggy patches now dry sponge, the streams, which had seemed perpetual, now stripes of bleached stones weaving down the valleys. The dogs were hard put to it to find a mouthful of water; their tongues lolled and their combined panting sounded like a marshalling yard full of tank engines. Human faces quickly turned to pink and then crimson as the morning advanced.

What of the grouse? They were there all right, in their old haunts: the peat hags and the heathery knolls up on the high ground. As predicted, there were a good many second broods and consequently a number of cheepers which we left for later in the year. Overall numbers were well down, partly the results of a high mortality on account of the overpopulation and under-shooting of last year and also of a mean spring. We found the remains of several dead ones. The grouse thrives only if populations are controlled correctly and moorlands carefully managed. Heaven help the bird and the wild country it inhabits if, for any reason, grouse shooting were to cease. Sheep and softwood plantations are a poor substitute for heather moors with their unique and fascinating wildlife communities. The keeper and grouse shooter are the bird's best friends. It is equally true that over-shooting, the advance booking of expensive days before proper head counts have been made, can be equally deleterious. There are places where what could once be described as grouse moors are now no more than hills covered with heather. True sportsmen moderate their shooting according to the numbers of birds on their ground.

We paused at the top to draw breath, straighten the line and off we went into the maze of hags, the crumbling peat cliffs, the wild country of the tops. I fancied I might be walking in places where the hand of man had never set foot (as the saying goes), but I crossed the bottom of a dried-out stream to be confronted, like Robinson Crusoe, by a solitary, substantial footprint, but unlike Man Friday's, this one was complete with Blakeys and cloverleaf nails. Even here, it seems, humankind came. Boundaries were as carefully recorded as on any southern arable farm. Ours was a series of white stones, carefully whitewashed from time to time as a polite reminder of just how far we were allowed to go. To cross one would be as unthinkable as to climb over a fence and shoot on a neighbour's farmland.

We located the first stone, swung to the left and followed the boundary on a long trudge round the top. The first covey rose, all well-grown birds. My neighbour and I managed to down a couple between us while the remainder, with a throaty cackling, fled over the next rise. Then there were shots from the far end of the line and a welcome rest while a runner was recovered. On we went, the odd singleton or covey exploding from our feet and scattering in the wind to provide sporting birds. One bird 'clapped' on the very place where my next footstep was to fall. Both dogs pointed the spot as well as any setters, but I could see not a feather, even in short, sparse heather, although I knew I was looking right at the bird. No.2 son tapped the spot with his stick and a single old grouse went clattering up, only to fall in a puff of feathers 25 yards away.

The next covey showed once more that dog often knows best. A bird fell dead, another separated from the covey, flew on strongly but collapsed and dropped 500 yards away. Master had not seen this but dog had and decided that the far one was the bird to retrieve first. Master sent it for easy one in front – dog set off for opposite horizon – master roared a command – dog carried on – dog went to the very point of the fall – dog retrieved a fine mature bird of the year, stone dead. Dog then proceeded to pick the second bird. There was a patter of applause from the gallery: man's emotions mixed, dog decidedly pleased with itself.

We paused for lunch (why is my end of the line invariably the furthest from the watering hole when a halt is called?) and basked in the sun reliving the events of the morning as we lolled on the springy heather. It was quite an effort, especially with big toe trouble, to heave myself back to the vertical and carry on. A snipe and fifteen brace in the bag were an incentive to push on for one or two more, and we were still a long way from home.

My old hero Drake is in his tenth year, deaf as a post and pig-headed; Kenzie, my two-year-old, is still headstrong. Shooting while trying at the same time to handle these two reprobates was not easy. It seemed as good a time as any so I handed the gun to No.1 son and told him to take my place while I walked with him

The pin-feather on a woodcock, the perk of the man who shot it.

and concentrated on the dogs. To say he leapt at the opportunity would be an understatement.

Within the first 100 yards a single grouse, not impossible at 15 yards' range and crossing slowly in front, gave him his chance, but even my kindly new open borings could not save a double miss behind. We went on into the next broken ground and a covey rose. The speed of his shots made me suspect browning, but one bird fell out, to be jubilantly retrieved by the whole Humphreys family plus dogs. That was good enough for a start, but as we were slogging through the bents on the homeward slope, a singleton rose 10 yards away. The first barrel missed – I crossed all my fingers, breathed a prayer, bit my lip and glared at the bird as it flew on; the second barrel had it bang to rights and it bounced on the tussocks. Both the boy and I knew that this was his first 'real' grouse and while no mention of browning had been made, we both celebrated this second bird in the manner which made explanations or recriminations superfluous.

The Woodcock is another exciting game bird, an inhabitant of the warm wood bottoms, of the damp heaps of rotten leaves and the muddy lower ends of fields. It is a medium-sized bird of the wader family with a long bill for probing in the mud for insects. It has rounded wings and large dark eyes, set high in its head. Its plumage is perfectly camouflaged for a life in the wood bottom or in the bracken and is of a mottled, speckled pattern of every shade of brown known to nature. Some nest in this country, but the majority which we see in winter have migrated westwards from Scandinavia and the Baltic. They make a landfall on the East Coast, often during the full moon in late October–early November. They are in a weakened state after their journey and they feed hard to recoup their strength. Then they continue their westward drift, settling in Cornwall or crossing the sea to Ireland, though woodcock may be found almost anywhere in the British Isles in season. Its habits are secretive and solitary, resting during the day in cover and feeding at night on earthworms and slugs. It nests on the ground in thick cover, and one of the miracles of bird life is the way the mother bird will take a newly hatched chick between her thighs and fly with it down to the nearest damp feeding place.

Woodcock tend to bring out the worst in shooting men who are normally models of care and safety in the field. It is such a prized bird to bag that the gun is especially eager to fire at it. It is a bird which takes some hitting, for it flies in a most deceptive zig-zagging flight, jinking between the trunks of trees, swooping down to land, popping out unexpectedly between the brambles. To hit one is no mean feat, and not for nothing is there a special, exclusive club run by *Shooting Times* to qualify for membership of which a gun has, in front of two witnesses, to kill a right and left at woodcock, that is, kill two with two closely consecutive shots. The solitary nature of the bird, the fact that it rarely flies in pairs and there is another gun nearby to shoot your second bird for you – plus the innate difficulty of the target, make this a rarely accomplished feat.

There is a hoary old tale of an ancient keeper who, when asked how he had managed to live for so long, replied, 'Because every time I hear the shout "Woodcock forward!", I throw myself face down on the ground.' Many a true word spoken in jest and the low, tempting flight coupled with the eagerness of the gun to bag the trophy can seduce a careful gun into taking a dangerous shot at a low angle or against a leafy screen behind which anyone could be lurking. If and when you are lucky enough to bag a woodcock, it is a pleasant and harmless little ritual to remove the pin-feathers and either stick them in your hat band or, as I do, in the shooting diary. The pin-feathers, one on each wing, are small stiff feathers, once much sought-after by artists for doing fine brush work. Remove the leading primary feather and the pin-feather will be visible poking out of the wing tip.

The Snipe is slightly smaller than the woodcock and is another bird hard to hit. It is a long-billed wader fond of soft, marshy places which it can probe for insects. A snipe will often fly up from your feet, uttering its rusty 'scape' of a call, and flicker away in a bewildering, darting, ziz-zagging flight. Walking-up snipe and shooting them well is definitely a knack achieved after considerable practice. Many guns display the old fault of shooting where the snipe has been instead of where it is going. After jinking, the snipe will often straighten out in level flight and, if it is still in range, that is the time to shoot. Some old timers would mutter a little rhyme such as 'Polly put the kettle on', before raising the gun.

Snipe may also be driven, but it is a chancy business persuading them to go in the right direction. All snipe shooting is best done on a windy day, for the birds tend to sit more tightly in such conditions. Like woodcock, snipe are truly wild birds and cannot be artificially reared, and there is little the keeper can do to encourage them except to keep some low, marshy land nicely damp to encourage them. These are two very exciting birds to shoot and the gunner who bags either can count himself a man with feathers in his cap.

The Mallard is probably the most shot member of the wildfowl family. It is a bird found in most countries of the northern hemisphere, a true globe-spanner, quacking sedately on a pond today, but tonight under the moon, up high on whickering pinions it is off to who knows where? Possibly to the Baltic, to Russia or up to the wild Northern firths. This has given all wildfowl a special appeal to the shooting man, for, apart from hand-reared mallard, they are truly wild, wary, fond of desolate and inhospitable tideways and marshes which have a strange fascination of their own.

The mallard is familiar from any village duck pond or park lake. The handsome drake with its glossy, bottle green head, purple-brown breast, delicate grey flanks, blue wing flash and black, curly tail is one of our most colourful as well as commonest British birds. Like most ground-nesting birds, the female is a uniform mottled, drab brown so that she is inconspicuous when on the nest. It is a gregarious bird, large flocks building up in autumn and winter while, in the breeding season, the drakes assemble as the ducks are incubating. It frequents a very wide variety of mainly still, shallow freshwater and brackish wetlands from large reservoirs to farm ponds, from sewage farms to rivers. It is also found on shallow estuaries and almost anywhere along the tideline. Its usual behaviour is to feed at night on farmland, on stubbles, frosted potatoes, acorns, beech mast and other rich foods. Mallard may be attracted to ponds by judicious scattering of corn (ideally, barley) in the shallows. The birds will flight in to feed at night and give good sport.

In September when stubbles are still plentiful, mallard feed on them in large flocks. A number of them will be birds of the year and these are especially good to eat. Now that walking-up partridges is out of favour and grouse shooting is so expensive, mallard in September mean the opening of many a shooting man's sporting year.

To the wildfowler there is a nice distinction between his sport and mere duck shooting. The latter may simply mean shooting reared mallard flushed tamely off a heavily fed pond which, in my view, does not accord with a spirit of true sportsmanship. The wildfowler finds his sport with wild birds down in the strange half land of the saltmarshes; usually he goes alone, pitting his wits against the wariest of birds in the most adverse conditions. The sport has its dangers, for treacherous tides can creep round behind you and cut you off; quicksands and soft mud can imprison you, while unexpected fogs and blizzards cause you to lose your sense of direction. Every year unfortunate wildfowlers are drowned or have lucky escapes. No one should venture out on a saltmarsh without knowing what he is doing. A compass is essential; a whistle, chart, torch and good bump of locality useful; an experienced companion is good sense.

Like other wildfowl, mallard can be responsive to decoys and to calling. Decoys should be set out on a flash of water, each one with a cord and lead weight to hold it in position. The precise species of the decoy is not important, for mallard will see the reassuring duck-like shapes down below and, enjoying the company of their own kind, they will fly in to land. Wildfowl have sharp eyesight, so the shooter must be well concealed and remain still while the birds are looking for danger signs. It goes without saying that you have chosen for your decoys a piece of water usually frequented by the birds and one on which they would be expected to land.

There are three basic calls for mallard which are easily mastered with a little practice. The attention-getter is the strident, high-pitched 'kaw, kaw, kaw'; the feeding chatter is a gutteral buzz, 'tacker tacker tacker tacker', and the seductive 'quack quack' is a female saying 'come hither'. Call only at specific birds, singletons or small groups and do not overdo it. It is no good calling hopefully at an empty sky and expecting mallard to come pouring in, while large flocks usually know very well where they are going and are not easily seduced by your quacking in the rushes below.

A mallard is a hard, fast flier, capable of great agility on the wing. It is a large, powerful bird and usually larger shot are called for to deliver the hard blow necessary to bring one down. Like many other game birds and wildfowl, mallard are usually missed behind, as the shooter has failed to estimate their speed properly.

Wigeon are another surface-feeding duck which feature in the wildfowler's bag. The wigeon is a migratory duck from Scandinavia and the USSR where it breeds on the tundra, arriving here in the autumn, building up to huge flocks in mid-winter. There is a small resident breeding population in Scotland and this shows signs of increasing and drifting south. The wigeon is mainly a grazing duck, showing a preference for cropped grass in water meadows or fields of winter-drilled corn. It was the bird of the mudflats, and flighting wigeon under the moon as they fly into a splash is a thrilling sport. The cock wigeon has an evocative, loud, whistling cry, 'wheee-ooo' which is unmistakable, and to hear it floating across the lonely wastes is a stirring sound. The bird is showing signs of changing its habits, roosting on inland waters and, like the mallard, feeding on surrounding farmland. The head of a cock wigeon is a striking chestnut and it has a lovely, sulphur-yellow forehead. Belly and undersides of the wings are snowy white.

The Teal and the pintail (see below) are the other two shootable duck most likely to be encountered. The teal is our smallest duck, remarkable for its quick and agile rise from a pond, from which it appears to spring vertically into the air like a rocket. When a spring of teal is fired at, the birds will divide and shoot off at a variety of angles, rather like a covey of grey partridge exploding over a hedge. Teal frequent much the same habitat as mallard, but on a shooting day there is the chance of one springing from the narrowest field ditch or muddy hole.

The Pintail is a handsome bird, the drake having two long pointed tail feathers which give it its name, and a dark, chocolate brown head with a thin white stripe. It too is a surface-feeding bird, but it does not feed on farmland as much as the mallard and wigeon, preferring freshwater marshes thick with weeds, the seeds of which form its principal diet. It is also fond of estuaries and mud flats, such as the Welsh Dee on which there is a very large overwintering population. A few pintail breed in the UK but it is mainly migratory, arriving in the UK from Scandinavia and Iceland in the autumn and departing in April.

There are other shootable British duck, but this thumbnail sketch of some of the commonest ones will give the beginner an idea of what duck shooting and wildfowling are about. It is important that you should be able to recognize the various species, for some of them are protected. Identification from a glossy picture in a bird book is one thing, but a half-seen shape flickering across the moon when you have only a second in which to make up your mind, is very much another. No two duck are the same, and with experience you will be able to distinguish the subtle differences of flight pattern, silhouette, call and distinctive features of each particular variety. The true shooting man and wildfowler prides himself as being an expert in such matters.

Wild Geese

Wild geese, especially the pink-footed goose and the greylag goose are the fowler's most sought-after quarry. They are the biggest by far of the shootable wildfowl, they inhabit wild places, the music of their babbling, wild calling is a most stirring sound; they are powerful, wary, fast and difficult to shoot. Keen fowlers will go to infinite lengths, travel great distances and incur considerable expense just for the chance of a shot at one of the great, grey birds of the uninhabited mosses or crawling tideways. The large, black and white Canada goose which nests, semi-tame, on ornamental lakes does not have the same appeal and while they may be shot as they flight in to feed on winter corn or grassland, when a fowler speaks of geese, he means grey geese.

The pink-foot has a sooty brown head and neck and pale brown-grey body with a white flash at the tail. The feet and legs are pink and the short bill is black with a pink band. It breeds in the sub-Arctic continent from East Greenland and Iceland to Spitzbergen, flying down the North Sea in great skeins to arrive in the UK for the winter. Flocks of geese are properly called gaggles when on the ground and skeins when they are airborne and may number several thousand birds; they make an impressive sight when they flight out of a bloodshot winter dawn or a wild sunset. They feed almost exclusively on farmland, grazing grass and young corn, feeding on barley stubbles and old potato fields. Even carrots (in Lancashire particularly) and greens are eaten. A large gaggle feeding regularly on a farmer's land can do a great deal of crop damage.

Old stubbles are popular with all geese. Note the white tail flashes on these greylags.

The Quarry

The greylag is rather larger than the pink, and is a uniform pale grey with bright orange beak and pink feet and legs. It is also a migratory goose with a similar range to the pink-foot, but there is a large and growing UK breeding population, nesting often in Scotland and never far from water. Its feeding habits are much the same as those of other grey geese.

Geese usually feed on farmland during the day and at night roost on a large loch, an inaccessible sandbar in the estuary or even on a calm sea. Under a full moon they will sometimes flight to the feeding grounds and may even spend the night on a quiet inland field. They are very nervous of predators, especially foxes, and are notoriously difficult to approach when on the ground. Rarely do they settle within range of a hedge or ditch behind which an enemy might lurk and when flighting in, they will fly high over a field and tumble in from a great height to land safely in the middle. When feeding, there are always some geese with their heads up, alert to approaching danger; one has only to give an alarm call and every bird is on the lookout. The next moment they have sprung aloft with great speed and agility for such large birds, and will be climbing up and away to safety, all clamouring as they go.

Some fowlers do not consider it sporting to stalk feeding geese, but others believe that the challenge of a long, difficult belly crawl is a legitimate part of the sport. There is no doubt that shooting geese on their roosting ground is very unsporting, spoils the sport of other fowlers and will, in time, drive the geese to seek a safer place. When flighting geese have crossed the tide line in the evening and reached the muds, they should be left strictly alone. In the old days, gunners would lie on their backs in shallow 'graves' right on the roost. This is no longer permitted by the fowling clubs who administer many of the foreshores; where it was tried, such as at Holkham and Wells in Norfolk fifty years ago, the geese completely abandoned the area, and only now are beginning to trickle back.

Geese should be shot either on morning flight en route to the feeding grounds, or in the evening on their way back to roost. The fowler will, by observation and local enquiry, have discovered the flight line and will hide himself somewhere on its length. This may be on the saltmarsh or on an inland field. If he has done his homework, the birds will fly over him in a number of ragged skeins. Usually they will be too high to shoot, but in times of violent head winds, blizzards or fog, they will be lower, battling along against the elements. It is then that the patient gunner might have a chance.

This lucky fowler with a goose in the bag is making the most of natural cover.

Another popular method of goose shooting is to decoy the birds on one of their feeding fields. The purist believes that this is faintly unethical and rightly claims that one goose shot on flight on the saltmarsh is worth five shot on a feeding field. Geese coming in to decoys can occasionally act almost suicidally and an unsporting gun might shoot a large number in a short time. However, it is not always so easy. The gun must first find the right field and this calls for local knowledge and some ground work; next he must beg permission to shoot, which these days is not readily given. Then he must be in position before dawn, well hidden, and with a dozen or more decoys deployed on the field. Goose decoys are bulky, so while the full-bodied polymer decoys are good, or even stuffed birds which some fowlers favour, there is a limit to the number that one man can carry. Hollow Shell decoys (from Shooting Developments of Fife) pack one inside another, are mounted on a patent peg which allows the decoy to rock gently in the breeze and look realistic. Each decoy is a good colour with the essential white recognition flash on the tail which is present in many gregarious birds and animals.

Even then, a change in the weather or farming disturbance can cause the geese to desert your field and go elsewhere, and you can only gaze in frustration at the distant skeins weaving across the horizon while the magic of their calling floats back to you on the wind. If they do decide to use your field, a call will often prove useful. Some of the great callers such as the late Mackenzie

Thorpe of Sutton Bridge, could call by mouth but this is a difficult art to acquire and demands a wide knowledge of grey geese to bring it to perfection. A good mechanical call is the OLT 88, or the Marshland goose call (Ralph Grant and Son Limited of Leicester): two different cries must be mastered. The first is the high-pitched, imperious 'pink-wink' of the pink-foot or 'ank-ank' of the greylag, the second the guttural feeding buzz which serves for both species. Mix the calls together and, as with mallard, call only singletons (which may be lost) or small parties. It is a waste of breath trying to attract the grand army which already knows very well whither it is bound and will not easily be diverted.

If all goes well and the geese respond to your decoys, wait until they are close before shooting. If in doubt, set a stick out in the field at ideal range and hold your fire until the birds have passed it. A goose on the wing is a very large bird; shooting pigeon and partridges will not have prepared you for a monster with a five-foot wingspan. One of the evils of goose shooting is out-of-range firing. The goose is a mighty bird, built to fly across oceans and continents and two or three pellets of big shot in a vital area are needed to bring one down. The vital area represents a very small proportion of the overall body outline. An X-ray scan of large numbers of grey geese carried out by the Wildfowl Trust in the 1950s revealed that almost half of the sample carried lead pellets somewhere in their bodies and yet were fit and well. Fowlers desperately eager to bag one, or mesmerized by those canopy wings into believing that the birds are within range, are guilty of trying hopeful shots. This is a slur on the sport: every spring there is a pathetic army of wounded geese left on the tideline, too weak or incapacitated to join their brethren on the long migration North.

Wait until the birds are well within range: forget the body and aim for the head. Large birds appear to be travelling more slowly than they really are, and they are so easily missed behind. If you are lucky enough to shoot six, exercise that most difficult human virtue, self-restraint, pack up and go home, leaving the later arrivals to drop in and feed in peace.

Inland goose shooting is now under considerable pressure. Many farmers are keen to have the geese kept off their grass and growing crops and they realize that fowlers will pay good money for the chance to come and shoot them. Some of these gunners think nothing of coming from the continent on the off-chance of a shot. This means that the shooting is no longer yours on request as once was the case. There are a number of guides who advertise their services in *Shooting Times* and who, for a fee, will take you out on fields where they have negotiated shooting rights; often they can also arrange your accommodation. This is a sensible option, but beware because there are some unscrupulous fellows in this market, happy enough to take your money, but not so hot when it comes to showing you geese. They have a cast-iron let-out, for they can claim (rightly) that goose shooting is a risky business and that nothing can be guaranteed. My advice is to go only with a guide on the personal recommendation of someone who has been with him before. A good guide will not shy at showing you his bag records or giving you the name of a satisfied customer whom you may contact for a reference.

The Whitefront, the other quarry goose, has not been mentioned yet. This is the rarest of the shootable geese, fond of fresh marshes and feeding on farmland. It has a delightful, laughing cry. The whitefront (of which there are two sub-species) is protected wholly in Scotland. The barnacle goose, the bean goose and the brent goose will be encountered from time to time on coastal marshes. All three are protected, although the barnacle may be shot on Islay under special circumstances. The penalties for shooting a protected bird are heavy, so it is all the more important that the goose shooter is an expert at bird identification.

Goose shooting, like all wildfowling, remains one of the most exciting forms of shooting. The fowler is thrown on his own resources, he goes to wild places in foul weather, he sees strange birds and sights denied the town dweller. His chances of a large bag are slim; often he will come home empty handed, yet some strange compulsion drives him out time and again on his wild goose chase. Once one is bitten by the bug, one is afflicted for life. I know men in their seventies who have been goose shooting for half a century, and still, on arthritic legs, they struggle out in the hope of a shot. Fowling represents a side of man's nature which supermarket technology is snuffing out of us.

I shot my first-ever goose on Boxing Day and every Christmas I allow myself a nostalgic wallow as I recall the occasion. I can see his head mounted on a shield and gazing reproachfully down upon me as I write. His beady eye which seems to hold that faintly censorious expression has little enough cause to rebuke me. He was a fine, old bird who had lived the anserine equivalent of three-score years and ten and he it was who, in a moment of absent mindedness, led his nine companions over the clump of frost-rimed Norfolk reed wherein I crouched.

I nearly did not go. Never had the bed seemed warmer as I

peeped through the curtains at a sky that was clear and at stars which glittered hard and sharp like diamonds on a Hatton Garden black velvet tray. A clear moon lit the roof tops and threw back a cold, ghostly reflection from the powdering of snow which two degrees of frost had turned to the consistency of powdered glass. No fowler would have blamed me had I snuggled back down between the covers and gone back to sleep like a Christian boy. Two thoughts kept me on my feet: one, I reflected that often in the past I had nearly not turned out, yet gone, and been justified in my decision; two, I was already out of bed and the hardest part of the early rising was over.

My bike skidded perilously on the frozen puddles, but at last I was safely at the marsh wall, sliding to a halt in the lee of some derelict farm buildings and concealing my machine in one of them where a broken-down Suffolk wain stood. Booted and armed with a long, brown-barrelled, single, magnum twelve, I stood shivering and felt the bite of frozen air in my nostrils. Ajax, my dog of the day who had already run two good miles behind me, skittered and danced, a pale ghost in a monochrome landscape.

I heard the distant bark of a dog on a lonely farm; a mallard quacked gently and a wigeon whistled. It was time to go, tinkling and crunching through filigrees of ice left by receding floodwater and as delicate as Nottingham lace. Every so often I would stop, hiss the dog to silence, hold my breath and listen intently before plodding onwards.

At last I came to one of my favourite spots, two miles up the marsh where a half-rotted gate-post leaned dangerously over some feathery reeds. An open stretch of water lay beyond it, now an ice-girt pool with a patch of open water in its middle. It looked as black as a puddle of ink beneath a half moon which swam through wisps of cloud as white as the cleanly cut segment of an apple. With a splash and a grunt of alarm, a string of mallard sprang from the water and became instantly invisible against the star-studded sky.

I waded out cautiously with my six decoys. The water was not deep but I did not care to slip and suffer a ducking on a morning such as that. My decoys were family heirlooms, hardy veterans, paintless and chipped but they had seen many a duck killed over them and some, judging from the pellet holes, from amongst them, and that long before I was born. They provided the reassuring black blobs on the water which incoming fowl might expect to see.

I draped some brown, frosted grass, flotsam from an earlier flood, onto the rushes to thicken my cover slightly. Even behind this flimsy screen I must have made a fearful, black figure hunched there in the gloom. Hopefully, when seen from duck's eye view, I would not have been so conspicuous. Ajax's quivering bulk shivered at my knee; we both scanned the skies like old-time air-raid wardens. The gun barrel felt blisteringly cold and the frost began to seep into my bones: ears and nose lost all feeling. I rubbed these extremities to restore the dull ache which proved they were still alive.

My hand was still in the act of massaging my ear when there was a flicker of wings and a silvery whistle across a pale dawn. A small knot of wigeon flashed across the curtain of cloud, vanished, reappeared and, with a whoosh, there they were on the water. My decoys seemed suddenly to have increased and multiplied. All at once, the real birds distinguished themselves; they relaxed and like clockwork toys began preening and dibbling. The nearest cock was not 10 yards away; he put up his head and whistled with surprising loudness, wheeeooo. . .wheeeooo. . . Ajax's eyes stood out like the proverbial chapel hat pegs as we both gazed, spellbound at this enchanting little cameo.

The sun had now edged above the rim of the far bank and the Christmas-cake landscape lost some, but not all of its ghostliness. Two mallard passed, a very possible chance on my left. As I peered around at them and half-shifted the gun barrel, my wigeon sprang and flew with a whistle and a growl. My finger was on the trigger, but I did not fire. To have broken the solemn stillness of the scene would have been like whistling in church, an unwarranted sacrilege by an unwelcome intruder. I left the picture undisturbed but vowed to return when the gales swept the marshes and roared in the withy beds – proper fowling weather when the atmosphere was less supercharged. In those conditions I could knock down wigeon with an untroubled mind, but not at Christmas-tide when they had settled so trustingly close to me.

What about that goose? To that I am coming, but the story, like all good tales, keeps its twist until the final paragraphs. I was tramping back along the marsh track, ready for a snipe or one of our little, wild marsh pheasants, should one show, and I heard a distant bugling in the sky. There, far away and as steady as a constellation, flew a line of ten geese. How distant and untouchable they seemed: if only they would come over and give me half a chance at them. Not much hope of that. By their height and steadiness of flight, they knew just where they were going and were hardly likely to fly near me, one tiny dot on miles of untenanted marshland.

But that is exactly what they did. For no reason that I could identify, those whitefronts turned at right-angles, lost height and, still going strong and not intending to land, made directly for me. Had I myself flown up and guided them, they could not have flown over that opportune clump of reed behind which I had sunk with greater precision. Ajax sat, good as gold, where I had dropped him, stock still in the open but his light coat blending with the icy tussocks. On and on came the birds: surely I would miss; might they turn at this last moment and save me the humiliation and agony of muffing such a chance? They would not. The gun found the shoulder, finger the trigger while the eyes ranged through that leading, wide black shape; forward . . . forward . . . forward . . . bang! There seemed to be an appreciable pause, just long enough for the heart to sink, the brain to say, 'missed', and the mind to beg for a second chance, but it was all right. There was a 'phrutt' of pellets striking pinions and, suddenly shrunken and aimless, my bird was falling for what seemed a full minute but was probably three seconds, and it thumped into the frosty grass with complete and exhilarating finality.

The head of that aged whitefront, admiral of the skein, mounted proudly on his shield, is the only stimulus I required to bring back that day with complete recall. Does not much of our love of field sports stem as much from what we remember as from what we do? Is not Christmas a proper time for such memories?

Pigeon shooting is a popular pastime, and many a shooting man becomes as addicted to it as the fowler does to his endless pursuit on the marshes. The woodpigeon is a common and familiar bird coloured a uniform dove grey with a pink breast, irridiscent neck patch, white collar and wing flash. It is found throughout the UK and shows a marked preference for arable land with woodland not far away. The pigeon's catholic diet makes it a serious agricultural pest, for it has expensive tastes, eating the best food at its most tender and vulnerable stage. Grain is popular, as are peas, beans, young brassicas, fruit, clover, ivy berries, acorns and beech mast. The pigeon is an energetic bird, and spends most of the daylight hours in search of food. It is gregarious and spends most of the year in large flocks which descend on growing crops in grey hordes and do considerable damage. It nests in hedgerow trees and bushes, making a flimsy nest of sticks and laying two white eggs. One pair may have a number of broods in a year and pigeons' nests with eggs have been found in every month, with peaks in May, June and July. Young pigeons have no white collar.

The pigeon's habit of feeding on the same field in large numbers for days at a time, make it the ideal bird for the decoyer. The shooter will have identified the feeding field by observation of bird movements and, having first obtained permission from the farmer, he sets up his 'stall'. A good squad of decoys, dead birds, polymer full-bodied models or the Shell pattern are set up in a realistic flock within easy range of the hide. Most birds feed head to wind, so set your decoys accordingly, and also place them as near a regular flight line as you can. The decoys should be about ten feet apart and set in a wedge shape with a patch of bare ground near the leading edge. This will tempt incoming birds to land in that area which, needless to say, is handily placed for your hide. Some full-bodied decoys may be placed in trees by means of a long pole: these are known as lofters. Another, usually a dead bird, may be set on a device called a wing-flapper: this has a cord running from it to the hide. When the shooter pulls the cord, the wings of the decoy rise and fall in a realistic manner, calculated to catch the eyes of distant pigeon which may not have noticed your static display.

There was a time when pigeons would come in boldly to decoys casually placed and unrealistic in appearance. The sight of what appeared to be a flock of their brethren feeding below was enough to draw them in to join the feast. However, decades of decoying and the making of heavy bags has made the pigeon more critical of decoy patterns and now these have to be of the highest standard of realism and carefully placed to be effective. No feathers scattered around, decoys roughly facing the wind, reasonably spaced and in places where pigeon might be expected to be are some of the tips.

The pigeon is a wary and keen-sighted bird, quick to spot a suspicious movement in the hedge or the pale flash of a human face peering out at them. Therefore, hides for pigeon shooting must be of a high standard. A pile of straw bales can be made into a perfect hide, often in the middle of the field right in the feeding area. More often, the decoyer has to make a hide in the nearest available natural cover. He must not cut into standing timber or hardwood trees, but may use elder or stunted bushes, chopping with a machete until he has made a cosy and well-camouflaged bower. This may be supplemented by poles and netting, but make sure that the netting blends with the background. Inside the hide the shooter must remain very still as birds approach, rising to shoot in one smooth movement only at the very last minute. He must look through and not over the leading edge of his hide, otherwise the pigeons will quickly spot him. Some sort of seat is useful, either a sawn-off shooting stick or the five-gallon drum

A modern pigeon shooter needs plenty of equipment.

which is especially popular. Camouflaged clothing and floppy hat are also important.

The modern pigeon shooter tends to travel heavy. In addition to his large bag of decoys, he should have with him a seat, some stiff wires to prop up dead birds for decoys, a machete or slasher for hide making, plenty of cartridges, poles and netting, his lunch and, of course, his gun. A large rucksack or army kit-bag is standard equipment. The time it takes to put out the decoys and to build a hide makes it important that the shooter has chosen the right place to start with; moving is not impossible but it is time consuming and may be avoided by five minutes' careful observation of the flight line. As in all shooting, pigeon should be addressed only when well in range. When a bird is shot it should, assuming no more birds are approaching, be set up with a wire beneath its chin and added to your decoy 'picture'. Like compound interest, the more decoys you have out, the greater the pulling power of your pattern, so make use of every bird. Do not leave any lying on their backs, for this will act as a deterrent and cause incoming birds to shy away.

Decoying pigeons is an art form and some shooters prefer it to all other forms of the sport. A pigeon can be a hard bird to hit in flight, resembling most of the other birds you are likely to encounter. It can be a high, driven pheasant one moment, a jinking woodcock, springing teal or flaring mallard the next. A gun who can regularly kill 50% of decoyed pigeons may count himself a very good shot indeed. The average is well below that figure.

The other traditional method of pigeon shooting is to wait in the roosting wood in the evening and ambush the birds as they fly in after a day on the fields. This sport takes place in early spring after game shooting has ended but before the pheasants have started nesting. The gun hides himself in the wood an hour or so before dusk; drab or camouflaged clothing is important if he is not to be spotted. As the pigeons fly in at treetop height he can enjoy some testing shooting, and the birds tend to come in with more confidence on a windy night. It is a frequently committed mistake to fire at the birds too early, at long range, when they are still doing their circling to check that the coast is clear. Invariably you miss and simply drive the birds away to roost elsewhere. Wait until they come well in and you will save cartridges and kill more birds.

One year, I remember, there had been a dry autumn and there was very little spring corn for the pigeon to go at; it had all been put in the ground months before. Farmers prefer to get their corn in early so that it has had a good start in life, ready to take full advantage of the mild weather of spring. This year had favoured that ploy, and the pigeon looked in vain for the drills crawling up and down and the sacks of seed corn and fertilizer stacked on trailers in the gateways. There were only beans to come, equally beloved of pigeon, but with a far lesser acreage than corn, there is

A large flock investigates a stubble.

that much less for them to go at. Bean seeds seem to be popular with all sorts of vermin. My own few rows of broad beans had gone into my garden way back in the February mild spell. I had soaked the seeds in paraffin but to no avail. When I went again a fortnight later, there was a neat hole over every seed where the mice had dug it out. They seemed not to have missed one.

On a somewhat grander scale, 15 acres of 'tick' or 'horse' beans had gone in at the end of the Parish lane. The ground was still a bit lumpy, but the farmer had to snatch a couple of dry days between showers. Lumpy soil means that the seed is not drilled so economically as it is into a fine tilth and a certain amount is scattered on the surface. This is what the pigeon like; they are not diggers like the rooks with pickaxe beaks, but will take only what they can see.

The foraging flocks soon found the field, and flew to an ash tree on the corner whence they trickled down like falling, grey leaves and began marching across the fields, a peck here and a peck there; a few hurrying steps and another stab over there. In a couple of days and at that rate they would soon clear the lot. Pigeon beaks have a degree of elasticity which allows them to swallow quite large objects: beans and even acorns seem to present them with no problem. Many shooters have recorded pigeon with over fifty acorns in their bulging crops. This greed seems to have a useful by-produce as this knobbly bag of acorns can act as a flak jacket or shot-deflector.

I lugged all my gear along the hedge to where I judged the flight line crossed and got my hide together. I used a variety of nets so as not to present too uniform a colour. Home-made jobs combined with West Dorset Kammo nets are a good team, and I use the excellent Ken Duglan telescopic hide poles to hold them up. A couple of cord braces fixed at each end to a hedgerow tree to stabilize the thing and you are set for the day.

For decoys, I also like a mixture of different sorts of artificials but I feel, as most decoyers do, that the dead bird is best of all although it is not always available. Today I had my favourite HH inflatables laced with some shells and a squad of the new polymer silhouettes out to one side: a good decoy that can be carried in large numbers without adding significantly to the bulk of your load must be worth consideration. In addition I set up my wing-flapper, a device in which I have come to have great confidence.

Pigeon were circling in ones and twos while I was still out on the field, running the flapper cord to the hide through a chink in the net. It felt just like the old, easy days of pigeon shooting, but no doubt they would clear off after the first couple of shots. I had barely settled on my seat and loaded the gun when one came, lilting slowly over my 'picture' and eyeing my landing stage with obvious interest. I stood up deliberately and an almost true cylinder barrel at 20 yards gave him no chance. At my shot, another bird clattered out from the blackthorn hedge to my left where, unbeknown to me he had settled during my preparations. I managed to get him too and he tumbled down, winged, into the dyke. Drake was out in a flash and had him to hand as I was in the act of setting up the first one on a length of stiff wire.

It was to be a good day and, despite my feeling rusty and out of practice, I found that in the first hour I had shot thirty-two pigeon for forty-one cartridges. Then the dreaded compacency set in and while I lost count of the statistics for the second hour, I know full well that my performance slipped. Thus is it always with me: I start well enough, fade and then pick up again later. Other shooters I know start badly and get better through the day as they relax and confidence grows; for others, things are the direct opposite. I expect that we all have our own patterns of performance in a day's decoying.

I need not have put up the wing flapper as the flight line came obliquely over my left shoulder so that the birds saw the decoys the moment they topped the hedge, swung round and beat in to windward to have a closer look. I gave the occasional pull on the string, more for the pleasure of seeing the thing work than anything, but on two occasions the distant speck of a pigeon, passing far off and almost unseen, half-closed its wings, checked, skimmed round and came whiffling down to provide me with an exhilarating hit. The shells seemed to be working and they looked attractive enough out on the black, peaty soil. As the numbers of the slain increased, gradually I took in all my artificials until, by lunchtime, I was left with a nice squad of about sixty dead birds and my flapper, set out before me.

Obligingly, the pigeon stopped coming at lunch-time allowing me to gulp coffee and snatch a sandwich without panic-stricken moments when, with a scalding cup half-way to my lips, an unexpected customer arrives. This is the usual pattern; so much so that for some, the pouring out of a cup of coffee from a flask has become a talisman which never fails to bring a bird. Today the birds were well-mannered and they gave me a quarter-hour respite. I was in the act of slipping the empty flask back into my bag when the next bird arrived – almost by arrangement, it seemed.

It was tea-time when the flight petered out and I was by then trying to guess how many I had down; had I made the elusive hundred? It surely could not be far short of that magic figure. I counted fifty into one sack and an equal number into the second, after I had dogged out the rest of the hedge and found a dropper, making a total bag of 101. I collected 137 cartridge cases in my rubbish bag after I had taken down the hide. Not every day does it take two trips to cart your bag back to the road. Time was when hundred-bird days were not unusual. Today new feeding and behaviour patterns, changes in agriculture and many more pigeon shooters make such an achievement cause for pride. I wonder how many days of poor bags it will be before I have another.

The pigeon has been described as the 'poor man's pheasant', a title which does it an injustice. Whether you are decoying or roost shooting the pigeon will challenge you to the full with its wariness, speed and power on the wing and the high standard of fieldcraft required to make a heavy bag. A gunner who thinks he has mastered pigeon shooting will not be found wanting with other quarry.

Rabbits and Hares Ground game, as rabbits and hares are collectively termed, call for a mention for they are both the cause for dangerous shooting. The simple fact that the gun is fired at a target at ground level as opposed to a bird up in the air makes hares and rabbits matters for special care. Often too, especially in the case of the rabbit bolting to or from a burrow, the shooter has the shortest time to make up his mind whether or not to fire. A swift snap shot at a rabbit in close cover can mean the peppering of a fellow-gun's ankles or the killing of a dog; both happen from time to time.

The disease myxomatosis, introduced from France in the 1950s, played havoc with the rabbit population, and resulted in the virtual disappearance of a form of shooting on which many a gunner had learned the craft. Rabbits have grown resistant to some strains of the disease and now there is a sprinkling of them throughout the countryside, but not like the numbers of the old days. An odd rabbit will still appear on a driven shoot, but often, for safety reasons, the rule 'no ground game' will have been given. What little rabbit shooting there is today takes place over ferrets or terriers which bolt the rabbits from their holes and give good snap shots as they dash to another bury or to the nearby hedge.

For safety's sake take the minimum essential number of people on a rabbiting expedition; the fewer the bystanders, the better. The shooter(s) should take up a position within easy range of the hole and where they can most easily intercept the rabbit's line of

A hare at full speed – big enough but easy to miss.

flight. Each gun must hold his position whatever happens, and not wander about and each must be absolutely clear in his mind as to the positions of other people present. When all is ready, the ferreter will introduce the ferrets and you stand by for action.

Shooting bolted rabbits is a knack; a well-fitting gun, small shot and open borings are a help, but a smooth mounting of the gun and swing past the rabbit's head are part of the answer. When shooting ground game your shot will throw up a cloud of dust or spray when it strikes the ground, so there is a ready indicator of where you are missing. Many shooters are amazed at just how far behind the rabbit this can be, for like most moving targets, rabbits are missed behind rather than in front.

The brown hare once so common on most farms has suffered a decline in recent years. The Game Conservancy is researching the reasons for this, but it seems likely that changes in farming practice lie at the bottom of it. Remember that, nowadays, it is virtually impossible to hunt any animal or bird to extinction and the depredations of the sportsman are as nothing when set against environmental changes or reduction of the habitat. There was a time when every village held an annual hare shoot simply to reduce the numbers which were damaging crops. Every able-bodied shooting man in the parish would turn up, and these occasions became a by-word for dangerous conduct, careless shooting and various sorts of accidents. Hare shoots are now much more infrequent, and some farmers have gone in the opposite direction and placed a moratorium on hare shooting to preserve the few they have left.

The hare shoot need not be a dangerous occasion, and I can think of some which are carefully controlled and where there is a high standard of safety. Expect to take your turn walking and standing. Wait until the hare is no further than 30 yards away before firing and put out a stick or a marker to help you judge the range. The hare is a large, strong animal, capable of great speed so it requires a hard, well-placed blow to bring it down. Long range or poor shooting means wounding and a hare can escape with most fearful injuries and that is a matter which no true sportsman would care to have on his conscience.

Some creatures come under the heading 'vermin' rather than true quarry species: some are on the borderline. The pigeon and the rabbit, for example, are pests to the farmer but valued sporting quarry for the shooter. We shall be looking in a later chapter at the enemies of game, but crows, stoats, rats, weasels and grey squirrels might all feature as items in the shooter's bag. All are common species, none is protected by the Law and the chance to shoot one should not be passed over. Make sure you know what you are shooting at: I make no excuse for repeating and re-emphasizing the importance of good identification.

Some keepers and farmers carry out night shooting to control vermin, rabbits especially. This is done from a truck or Landrover with a powerful, hand-held spotlight and a shooter on the back. Rabbits will be mesmerized by the beam and may easily be shot. This is a dangerous activity and should be done only by very experienced shooting men and not by novices. Also there are strict laws which apply to night shooting, written authority to be sought, locals and the police to be informed and other arrangements made. If you have the chance to go as an observer, then accept and see how it is done, but leave the shooting to older hands until you have become proficient.

One final point about safety: it has been made before and I make no excuse for repeating it. Make sure that your gun handling is faultless from the safety point of view; expect to be rebuked in no uncertain terms if you make a mistake. By the same token, do not fear to grasp the nettle and speak out if you should find yourself looking down the barrels of someone's gun or sense the pellets whizzing dangerously close to you. If you are too polite to make a fuss, you are doing no one a service and might be responsible for the offenders' being involved in a serious accident at a later date. Do, however, be discreet, for no one likes a prig, especially a young one! Do not become paranoic about it nor speak loudly about what you consider to be every little slip by your fellows; a quiet word at the right time and in the right place is more than enough.

As well as becoming an expert at quarry and non-quarry identification, you must know precisely what are the shooting seasons for each of them. These vary from bird to bird and, in the case of wildfowl, are different on the foreshore from inland. It is worth learning them off by heart; the information is useful in quizzes apart from anything else, and you will be surprised at how many supposedly experienced shooting men are vague on the open seasons of some of the obscurer birds.

SHOOTING SEASONS

all dates are inclusive

Pheasant	1 Oct to 28 Feb
Partridge	1 Sep to 1 Feb
Grouse (Red)	12 Aug to 10 Dec
Grouse (Black)	20 Aug to 10 Dec
Capercaillie	1 Oct to 31 Jan
Ptarmigan	12 Aug to 10 Dec
Woodcock (England and Wales)	1 Oct to 31 Jan
Woodcock (Scotland)	1 Sep to 31 Jan
Snipe	12 Aug to 31 Jan
Golden Plover	1 Sep – 31 Jan
Wildfowl	1 Sep to 31 Jan
(duck and geese)	above and on the foreshore

– but there is an extension of twenty days for these birds to 20 Feb below high-water mark of ordinary spring tides. The only shootable wader is the golden plover, 1 Sep to 31 Jan. Shootable geese are Canada geese, greylag geese, pink-footed geese and whitefronted geese, the last named in England and Wales only. Shootable ducks are mallard, wigeon, teal, pintail, tufted, pochard, shoveller, gadwall and golden eye.

Brent, barnacle, cormorant, shag, goosander and red-breasted merganser may be shot only under special licence if one can prove that they are doing damage.

You must become an expert at quarry identification.

9
The Amateur Keeper

I hope that, by now, the reader has gained the impression that there is far more involved in shooting than an indiscriminate pulling of a trigger. To become a good, proficient shooting man you have to become an expert in a number of fields: ballistics, quarry identification, the law, marksmanship, choice and care of equipment and others. Possibly most important of all is a wide general knowledge of the countryside, of the farming calendar, of country people and the daily and seasonal affairs of the woods and fields. There is a section of society currently looking closely and often with hostility at country sports, some of which are suffering from regular orchestrated attacks in the Press and elsewhere. Carrying a gun and using it responsibly is both a right and a privilege; abuse it by wounding, by shooting protected birds, by killing too many easy wildfowl over decoys and you will rightly attract criticism from the general public as well as from more sporting colleagues.

Shooting has an important part to play in country life. It represents a proper harvest, fairly taken, of common species which, if left to their own devices and deprived of the sportsman's protecting hand would rapidly diminish to the point of extinction. In whose interest is it to remove industrial pollution from rivers? The answer is the angler who is quick to defend his waters and to prosecute those who seek to foul them. By the same token it is the shooting man who sees that covers are planted for his birds, that wetlands are not drained, that vermin is controlled and that grain is scattered during the cold winters. His interest in his sport and desire to see healthy stocks of game birds in the autumn is the biggest single incentive to see that this is done. Shooting men of our grandfather's generation planted many of the woods and spinneys which now delight us. We are responsible for passing on a countryside just as rich if not richer in wildlife so that our own descendants may have the pleasure of it.

Thus, every shooting man must also be a conservationist at

heart. The Game Conservancy has organized a massive research project, financed largely by the farmers themselves, to find out how intensive cereal growing may be made compatible with game birds – partridges especially. Spraying tactics, more selective weed and insect destruction and the preservation of nesting habitat all form a part of the picture. They have established, for example, that to leave one strip on the outside of a corn field unsprayed can increase partridge chick survival by 300%. The insects on which the birds depend are spared by this tactic with an insignificant effect on the crop yield. Not for nothing did the Wildfowlers Association of Great Britain and Ireland (WAGBI) change its title to The British Association for Shooting and Conservation (BASC) for it had realized how important it was that the two concepts of Shooting and Conservation should be seen to be linked.

Every shooting man has a small part to play and being a member of the BASC is essential, for that is a tangible way of putting a tiny bit back into a sport which has so much to offer you. If you are lucky enough to have your own little place on which to shoot, there is much that you may do to improve it and have fun at the same time. Put out of your head the idea that a game shoot must be at least 2000 acres and have three keepers to run it. All you need to shoot on is one field, a patch of rough ground, some boggy bottom land where you may beg or buy permission. I know a first-class shoot in East Anglia on which to kill a hundred birds a day is the norm, but which is only 68 acres. I know of another in Hampshire which has 11 acres and provides good sport.

The owners of these two little patches have made them into havens for game. The first essential, especially for pheasants, is to have cover in which they may shelter from the wind and hide from prying eyes. Tall trees are not suitable as the protection is needed down at ground level. Fir trees or ground-hugging shrubs are ideal. A wise farmer will be happy for you to plant one or two here and there in wasted spaces, but you must ask him first. It will surprise you how small an area it requires to hold a pheasant in winter or a nest in summer. Most of your shooting will come from the crops such as sugar-beet or stubble which the farmer grows, but again, a strip of mustard, the seed scattered by you by hand, on a stubble which is not to be ploughed will make very good cover until the frosts cut it down. On the shoot which I run we make it a rule to plant a few quick growing firs every year so that, over a period of years, the habitat improves. I repeat that permission must be asked before you do any planting.

Elder bushes make good cover and if you have any, these should be partially cut through with an axe and bent down to the ground.

They will continue to grow, but will put out fresh shoots from the bole, giving your birds protection where they need it, at ground level. Persuading the farmer that it would not affect his crops if he left that weedy bank unsprayed or the farm track verges unmown are valuable ploys. You will gather that the farmer is a key figure in the habitat equation. Some will be more sympathetic than others, but I suspect that most of them would prefer to see their land looking pleasant with trees and cover to a featureless crop-producing factory – provided the yield of the farm is not noticeably affected. Think of it that every bush, each nettle, clump of weeds and hedge bottom is habitat for game; treasure, protect and enhance each one of them.

The second important keepering task which anyone may do on his shoot no matter how small or humble, is to control the vermin. Like weeds in a garden, vermin will flourish at the expense of the more desirable inhabitants of the countryside. If left to their own devices they will multiply, songbirds and game will dwindle and all your other keepering jobs will be in vain. Creatures the keeper calls vermin fall into two main categories, ground vermin and winged vermin. Winged vermin comprises members of the corvid family, mainly crows, magpies, jays, jackdaws and, to a lesser extent, rooks. The carrion crow is top of the list, for it is cunning, sharp-eyed, evasive and long lived. Its pickaxe beak will deal with eggs and chicks in a ruthless manner, picking them off one at a time until the last one has gone. They quarter the fields like setters looking for nests, their sharp eyes will spot most of them, especially in April before the cover has grown.

A fox on a shooting day – an enemy of game, but another man's sport.

It is illegal to leave poison baits lying around, a practice which is indiscriminate and dangerous. Many a good dog and bird of prey has been killed by taking baits left for crows; severe penalties fall on those who are caught transgressing. The crow is best shot at its nest, the shooter waiting patiently and perfectly concealed at the foot of the tree. The second of the pair may take more time; crows mate for life and are even more cautious of returning to the nest when they suspect all may not be well and when they hear no answering 'caw'. The dead crow or a decoy sitting near a dead rabbit on the field near your hide will sometimes draw in a crow, for they are also inquisitive birds. Supplement your decoy with some gentle calling and you might just be lucky. In America, crow shooting is considered a sport in its own right.

Check your shoot for nests; they are usually conspicuous, but do not make the mistake of shooting at the nest itself. Nothing short of solid ball or slugs will do it the slightest damage for the deep cup is placed to be safe from such attacks. You will disturb the nest only enough for the crows to desert, and their new nest might not be so easy to find, and could well be over your boundary. In winter, crows in flocks will roost in favourite woods: they may be ambushed as they fly in at night. Rooks are less trouble, eat many harmful insects and weed seeds, but also some corn and the odd partridge egg omelette. However, rooks are having a hard time what with their favourite nesting trees dying through Dutch elm disease and their numbers only just holding their own. It is the bird of the English village, of the vicarage rookery, and it would be sad to see it suffer further.

All hawks and owls are protected by law, and there are severe penalties for those who harm them or take their eggs. To say as much should be sufficient, but I ought to add that most raptors, from the tiny kestrel to the golden eagle, will take game birds as part of their diet. Raptors have suffered badly in recent years thanks to pesticides, illegal falconers and egg collectors and only now are they showing signs of a revival. To have one on your shoot should be considered an honour and you should be happy for it to take the occasional game bird. The principal diet is more likely to be rabbits, rats and moorhens, all quarry easier to take than game birds so leave all raptors strictly alone and enjoy sharing the countryside with them: they have as much right to be there as you.

Jays, magpies and jackdaws may be thinned out, especially in spring when they are nesting. Make it a habit to take a gun with you on your spring rounds, and deal with the vermin active at this time of the year.

Ground vermin includes rats, stoats, weasels and, in some parts of the country, mink. Game birds are, as we have seen, ground nesting and their eggs are vulnerable, as are the chicks in their first few critical days of life. Ground vermin will hunt the hedges and ditches, finding the nests and sucking the eggs one at a time. A hen pheasant or partridge will often be bold in the defence of her nest but usually her efforts are of no avail. When the hen is still laying her one egg a day and leaving the nest between times, ie before she has begun to incubate, the clutch is especially vulnerable to wandering stoats.

The standard equipment for dealing with all these varmints is the Fenn trap set in a tunnel in a regularly used run. Vermin has regular paths, usually alongside hedges or ditches. Where two cross, or a farm road bisects a hedge, is a busy place, and a practised eye will be able to see the path the stoat will take as he darts across. Ground vermin has a passion for dark holes and tunnels, so the trapper will construct an artificial tunnel either by re-arranging what nature had provided in the form of logs or he will place a porous land drainage pipe, which a stoat will be unable to resist. This will lead him straight to the concealed trap, a device which is Ministry approved and, if properly set, is an instant killer. The old-fashioned gin trap was more likely to catch a creature by the foot and, while there are still a good number of them to be found in sheds, they have been outlawed for some years.

Set your traps round the boundary of your shooting ground on the principle that you will intercept vermin on its way in from outside and maintain a vermin-free zone inside. Traps must be checked at least once a day, there just might be a wounded creature caught, and even a rat deserves a quick death. Moreover, a sprung trap is no longer working for you and the beauty of a trapping line is that it is operational for twenty-four hours a day. Place your traps near easily accessible points; make the vermin come to the trap. There is no point in having to walk the length of two fields to check a trap when you could, just as easily, set it nearer the roadside. Stoats and weasels will travel considerable distances in April and May when they are really on the move and are as likely to be caught in this end of a long hedge as the other.

Experience and practice will make you a competent trapper, for it is not a difficult art to learn. The tunnel should look natural, be set in a vermin run, should have no whiff of after-shave or tobacco on it and the Fenn itself be carefully concealed. Some human passers-by will take and destroy your traps, not understanding their purpose or simply to be a nuisance, so do not make the site of a trap too obvious to human eyes.

Badgers are rare enough to make their depredations of the

occasional nest a matter of little account; hedgehogs are a confounded pest and will kill the hen and take the eggs as boldly as the most bloodthirsty stoat. Unfortunately, the hedgehog is a protected animal since 1981. The fox is a serious predator of nesting game for he too will take the sitting hen as well as the clutch so you have lost part of your breeding stock. At least when a crow steals the eggs the hen will lay a second brood. Remember that the fox is a vital element in another man's sport; all field sportsmen ought to be brothers and if the hunt comes across your shooting ground, it does not do for every fox to have been exterminated. However, if your land is not hunted or if you have a plague of foxes, you will never have a good head of game. I have seen fox earths stuffed with remains of pheasant, partridge and mallard, mostly females and mostly taken off the nest. That single earth had accounted for enough game to last a man a whole season.

Poison baits for foxes are also illegal, so foxes must be shot or snared. Fox drives in spring through woods, spinney and rough, grassy banks are standard practice on many shoots. Fox earths with cubs should be gassed there and then with Cymag gas. This is dangerous stuff and can kill a human so find out how to use it, go accompanied and do it *now*. Once you have looked at an occupied earth, the vixen will move the cubs that very night to a place which you may never find, so do the job immediately.

Snares must now be free running and not self-locking (Wildlife and Countryside Act 1981) and should be set in any likely run, firmly anchored to a heavy but movable log. Plank bridges over ditches, obviously used gaps in hedges or along the headlands of fields are the favoured places. Most snarers set the loop of a snare too high; set it with the bottom no more than nine inches from the ground, and be certain to check it at least once a day. If you know you are likely to be away from home for a few days, all snares and traps must be sprung, unless you can find a reliable person to keep an eye on them for you.

Early spring is the time to set your traps, and there is no reason why they should not remain down all year. For no obvious reason some places are regular and excellent catchers, while others which look just as good, remain empty. Leave a skeleton staff of traps down all year, for every rat and weasel they catch, is one less to trouble you next spring. Old keepers would establish what they called a gibbet, a rogues' gallery of their victims hanging on a bush. This showed their employers how vigilant they were as trappers, but today such a practice is considered outmoded. It gives offence to some country users, and remember that there are others besides yourself, who may come suddenly upon this ghastly

sight. Record every head of vermin killed, by all means, and also
the place it was caught for, in that way, you will see patterns
beginning to build up, but bury the bodies discreetly.

Old keepers claimed that no shoot could build up and maintain
stocks of wild game while the vermin was allowed to run riot. The
young shooter must assume the habit of recognizing the enemies of
game and deal with them accordingly every time he meets one.
Cats are a vexed matter, for a domestic tabby run wild is a fearful
game killer, but this does not give you licence to bowl over each
and every cat you meet. There could be some unpleasantness if, on
a shooting day, you proudly presented your host with the corpse of
his wife's prize Siamese: such things have happened. It is best, in
the early days, to leave cats to more experienced hands.

Feral mink are a fearful pest, the perfect game killer, equally at
home in the water and climbing trees. Like a fox, it will kill for
bloodlust. Mink may be caught in tunnel traps set along water-
ways, or in a special cage trap designed for the purpose. Every
head of vermin brought to book is a nest or two saved, and that
thought must serve as an incentive to the amateur keeper to do as
thorough a job as he is able.

The other essential area in which the shooter may improve his
sport is by feeding in hard weather. Game birds will stray away
from your ground if there is no food to hold them there; the bad
times are not the autumn when the whole countryside is a
storehouse, but in December, January, February and early March.
Establish a number of feeding points round the shoot, usually in
patches of cover or woodland. Grain, beans or acorns are beloved
by game birds, pheasants especially, and they will grow accustomed to finding a supply at the same place every day.

To make a feed stack simply pile the food in a pyramid on the
ground and thatch it over with thin sections of a straw bale. This
will keep out the weather and prevent sparrows from stealing your
precious grain. Most cereal farmers will spare a keen shooter the
sweepings from the corn bins, or unthreshed ears from the dresser;
these may be eked out over a surprisingly long period. Another
popular method is to suspend a five-gallon chemical drum from a
branch so that its bottom is about 14 inches from the ground. Fill it
with grain, fit a watertight lid and punch holes or slits in the
bottom and the birds will be able to help themselves. Some feeders
may be made of 40-gallon drums, more trouble to put together
than the smaller ones, but they hold eight times as much and
require filling less regularly.

All feeding places must be accompanied by rat baiting points
otherwise rats will steal most of your precious grain. Do not

begrudge finches and tits a few grains, for by feeding and improving the habitat, you are making the countryside better for other creatures as well as game birds. Grain may be scattered along hedge bottoms and made available at any place where game birds are likely to congregate. It is easy enough to do, but it does call for a regular commitment and a certain amount of hard, physical work. If you have fed your birds well, late in the season and into March, they will not only feel less inclined to stray, but will arrive at the next breeding season in good shape for the rigours of egg laying and incubating.

Modern methods have brought home rearing of a few game birds to within the scope of anyone who has a patch of lawn. The principle of putting back into the countryside something of what you take out is a sound one, for often it seems, that there are more shooters than there are things at which to shoot. A rearing programme need not be vast; twenty birds or fewer will give a great deal of interest and pleasure and teach many lessons about the habits of game. Pheasants, mallard or red-legged partridge are good birds to practise on, as all are relatively hardy and easily obtainable.

The whole process is one of stages, beginning with the incubation of the eggs, which you may do either in an electric incubator or with a broody bantam. A broody is ideal if you can find one, as she will see the chicks through to maturity. Incubators holding a hundred eggs are easily available, but if the funds allow, try to buy one which turns the eggs automatically, for this can be a chore to do by hand, three times a day. When the chicks hatch, they require

Home reared pheasant chicks – easily kept on most back lawns.

warmth, especially at night, which they would usually derive from the mother's feathers. A gas, paraffin or electric brooder in a round pen of cardboard will see the chicks through the first, critical few days. The pen should be round, for chicks are foolish birds and will jam in piles in the corners of square or rectangular cages and suffocate.

Feed the chicks on turkey crumbs in the early days, and see that they have a plentiful supply of clean water in patent drinkers to prevent the birds from fouling it or drowning in it. Move the pen from time to time to keep onto clean ground for a dirty pen bottom is a breeding ground for diseases. The poults may be removed onto the lawn, after about a week, provided the weather is good, but the artificial heat must still be available and the birds moved under it and penned in at night, safe from draughts and predators.

Once the pheasants or partridges are about eight weeks old, they should be hardy enough to manage without extra heat, which will gradually have been phased out; they will also be eating full-sized grower's pellets. Some of the cock pheasants will already be showing their colours. Then comes a critical stage, releasing the birds on your shoot. Make a wire pen like a large hen run which encloses a patch of your good cover; pull out the leading wing feathers of one wing on each poult which is painless and more effective than clipping, and release them in this pen. If you have not the resources or space to make a permanent pen, a series of sections 8 feet by 4 feet tied together at the corners to enclose the largest possible area is a good enough substitute. Cover the roof with fine mesh nylon netting such as gardeners use to protect strawberries.

The idea is that your birds will gradually become accustomed to life in the wild and will come to regard the release pen with its supply of food and water as home, staying round it for the whole winter. Birds in the release pen are easily predated, and a fox or a mink might kill the lot in one night. There is no certain way to prevent it, but do your spring vermin work well to reduce stocks and set snares and traps round the pen. Leave the fence wire floppy rather than tight to prevent a fox from scrambling over it and make sure there are no gaps at ground level, for a stoat can squeeze through the tiniest chink. Wean the birds onto corn – it is cheaper than pellets and it will become their main diet anyway; then after two or three weeks in the pen, allow them to leak out into the surrounding farmland. A full-time keeper would dog them in twice a day, but unless you live near the shoot, this is probably too time-consuming. The birds should return to the pen area in the evening and will supplement your wild stocks.

Rearing can be fun, but it takes time and is not essential. The philosophy that if you shoot ten then you also rear and release ten is a good one, but remember that the wild bird is the cheapest and usually the best. Wild birds make better mothers, are less likely to stray, fly better and know their way about the shoot better than reared ones.

If you are lucky enough to be allowed to help the local full-time keeper, you have a golden opportunity to learn the craft from an expert. Many do not have this chance, but must learn from books, courses, and from talking to other shooting men. The current major development in the game shooting world is the 'Do It Yourself' shoot. Small teams of enthusiasts are renting what often may appear to be unpromising pieces of land, building up stocks of game by applying the three basics of habitat, vermin control and feeding, and enjoying cheap sport. What is more, they have a great deal of fun doing the various jobs and seeing the place improve as a direct result of their management. The young shooter should, as soon as he has passed his apprenticeship, try to join such a syndicate, for this is the way that field shooting is going and where most of the sport of the future lies. The ranks of gamekeepers, sad to say, dwindle by the year. All their expertise and skill together with their massive contribution to the countryside is going with them. To employ a full-time keeper is an expensive business, as is to fund the large rearing programme which is a large part of the modern keeper's round. Sadly a growing number of estates are finding the outlay does not reflect the return. As the keeper's star sinks, that of the DIY, amateur keeper rises, and this is the one on which the newcomer should fix his gaze.

The shooting man who arrives on a shooting day familiar with the layout of the shoot, who has planted with his own hands some of the trees, lugged sacks of corn over muddy fields, given of his time and energy to traps and agonized over a dozen pheasant chicks in his garage, will be the man who derives most from shooting. He who turns up on the day with no interest in the wider implications of shoot management, but who expects to be driven to a peg, have his gun handed to him and then shoot at clouds of driven pheasants which he regards as little more than so many animated clay pigeons, is a man who takes his pleasures sadly.

Last season on our shoot, a gun shot a fine cock pheasant, one of the best shots of the season. It was found to be wing-tagged, and the gun who shot it had reared the bird from an egg three years before. It was flushed from a wood we ourselves had planted: one of us had fed the bird, another trapped its enemies. As in much of life, you may take out of it only as much as you put in.

134

10
Gundogs

For anyone who intends to become a serious shooting man a dog is a necessary adjunct to his equipment – it is also very much more than that. I have remarked that the eye of the public is currently very much on the field sportsman and one of the uses of a dog is to find wounded game. Even the best shot will not kill cleanly every time, and a pheasant with a broken wing may fall emphatically enough to earth, but go to the place and it will have vanished. Pheasants and partridges are ground-dwelling birds, fleet and strong of leg and, even when wounded, they can outrun most humans. A wounded bird will set off running like a stag the moment it hits the ground and may travel two or three fields before stopping.

When it does stop, it will hide in an inaccessible place where it cannot be easily seen, sometimes down a rabbit hole, in the depths

A labrador heaves himself up a vertical bank to bring home the bacon.

of a dense bramble patch, down a drainage pipe or beneath a jumbled pile of wood. No human being has a hope of chasing and recovering such a bird, so it is left to die a sad death, the bird is wasted, and the public image of shooting takes another knock.

Similarly, a duck will dive in shallow water, make its way, half-submerged, to the bank and lie like a stone in the thickest cover – again, no human eye can detect its presence.

In a third instance, a bird may fall beyond an unjumpable ditch, out of view behind a drystone moorland wall, or on the wrong side of a tall hawthorn hedge. The shooter must then walk a considerable distance to a bridge or point to cross the obstacle, and walk back on the other side until he is level with the spot from which he shot, and hunt in what might be thick undergrowth until he finds the bird. On another occasion a bird may fall stone dead but land in a field of roots, a long stubble, a bed of nettles or a reed bed. All tend to be featureless and to find even a dead bird on such ground can be surprisingly difficult and time-consuming. In my earliest, dogless days with the gun, I would fix my eye on the spot, walk directly to it, drop a handkerchief and walk slowly round the point, searching diligently. Even then I lost the odd bird and had no chance whatever of picking a runner.

All these situations, which occur sometimes hourly in the shooting field, call loudly for the services of a dog. Even a poor dog is better than no dog. A dog with even a whiff of gundog in him will pass through the hedge, leap the ditch, sniff in the sugar-beet and find the dead bird, which is most of the battle. Persuading the dog to then retrieve the bird to hand is not too difficult a task. Game, especially when wounded, has a scent attractive to dogs but imperceptible to the human nose. The dog has a chance of tracking and retrieving a running, wounded bird which has left a strong scent on the ground as it passes. Some dogs do this better than others, and much of their innate ability may be enhanced by breeding, training and experience.

In an earlier chapter I mentioned the importance of the role of the picker-up on the driven shoot; no shoot should operate without at least one. His job is to pick up birds which have been hit but have the strength to pass well beyond the guns and land in cover far behind them. A good pair of pickers-up will retrieve possibly twenty such birds from a bag of a hundred head, and they take a pride in picking every one of them. They will be seen as distant figures patiently working a hedge on the far side of sixty acres of heavy plough and not picking up obviously dead birds lying on open ground within a few yards of where the guns are standing. Some shooting men, often those who have seen their share of sport, may come to prefer picking up and working their dogs to shooting. This is also a way that shooters, who tend usually to be male but by no means always so, may encourage wives, sisters and girl friends (but not all at once) to share their sport. Women often make better dog-handlers than men.

The other important job of the all-round gundog is that of a game-finder and flusher. Pheasants especially will run, hide and creep into dense brambles or lie like stones beneath the sugar beet leaves within a few feet of where a human blunders by; they will not give a hint of their presence. Thus, much game is 'walked over' by dogless guns and the amount of shooting they may expect is strictly limited. Again, the amazing nose of the dog will hunt them out and push them onto the wing. A good dog has no fear of prickles but will thrust a questing snout into the sharpest thorn bush and push out a wily old cock pheasant which has sought sanctuary there.

All this is as it should be with good dogs, but many dogs one comes across are less than perfect and, like their masters, they exhibit their shortcomings for all to see. For example, a hunting dog which works on its own with no reference to its master and chases running pheasants and partridges through the cover, is not a popular shooting companion, for it will flush most of the birds out of range. The retriever which on its own initiative runs off to fetch a bird before the word of command can also be a nuisance on a formal day and divert approaching duck or geese when out fowling. There are times when a quick retrieve is desirable. Dogs which whine when waiting for birds to approach, which fight other dogs, which crush game in their teeth instead of delivering it gently, which drop runners prematurely, allowing them to escape or which have an innate fear of thick cover or water are certainly less than ideal, but there are numerous dogs which have one or more of these vices and yet are still far better than no dog.

In Victorian times, the well-to-do shooting man could afford to maintain a kennel of various specialist gundogs. He would have his pointers and setters for grouse shooting and walking up partridges, clumber spaniels for woodcock shooting in the oak woods, Irish water spaniels for wildfowling, non-slip retrievers for his driven game shooting, terriers for ratting, everyone an expert for each limited field of shooting. He would also have at least one man to look after them. Times have changed and the modern shooting man has not the room, let alone other resources to maintain a large kennel, so he has one gundog which combines as many of the necessary skills as possible. The general-purpose dog should be able to swim, hunt, flush, retrieve, have no fear of thick cover, have a kindly disposition and be easy to train. The modern dog may spend some of its time in the house so must be good with children, while modern man with his busy life has less time to spend on training than once he did.

Two major breeds have emerged and evolved as the all-in-one modern gundog, namely the labrador and the springer spaniel. There are still, and it is good that there should be, enthusiasts for the old breeds so that pointers, Irish water spaniels, cocker spaniels and the others are preserved and worked in the field to delight us. However, nine out of ten shooting dogs are either labradors or springers. Both breeds combine most of the qualities we require, but each has a slightly different emphasis. The Springer spaniel is an expert at hunting and flushing, showing no fear of fierce prickles, always bustling about, keen to investigate every clump of grass in case there might be a bird in it. The labrador is rather less highly strung and is traditionally used to retrieve shot game, walking to heel during the shooting or sitting by a peg on a driven day and, on command, running out to retrieve game, dead birds or runners, which may fall. However, springers will retrieve well and labradors can be trained to hunt and flush.

Both dogs are what is known as ground scenters, tracking the path of game which has run by following its scent on the ground. The pointers and setters are air scenters which hold their noses high to catch the scent of game borne to them on the wind. When a

A hare is a large mouthful, even for a labrador.

pointer works up to a covey of grouse squatting in the heather, it will 'freeze' in a statuesque, pointing position with one fore-paw raised. Dog and birds will stare each other out, each waiting for the other to make the first move, and giving the gun time to walk close enough to have a shot when the covey eventually rises. However, these, as we have seen, are specialist breeds and they are not good in water or rough cover, nor are they supposed to retrieve.

The learner-shooter will, sooner or later need a gundog. Buying a puppy is the easiest part of the job. You must have sleeping accommodation, a run, a supply of food, a body of training knowledge and, most of all, the realization that twice a day, seven days a week, 365 days a year for the next twelve years or so, you have an obligation to feed, exercise and look after the animal. You must make arrangements for it to be cared for when you are away from home, see to it in sickness and in health (all those vets' bills), groom it and allow it to take over a large part of your life. In return, you will have a constant shooting companion, a bag-filler and a friend whose deeds will fill you with fierce pride one moment and deep shame the next. When it misbehaves in public you wish the ground would open and swallow both of you up, but should it make a good retrieve of a strong runner which may have beaten other dogs, you will feel that life has little more to offer.

When you have decided that you have the time, the facilities and the opportunities to take on the responsibilities of dog ownership you choose your puppy from one of the advertisements in *Shooting Times* or from someone known to you locally. Be sure your puppy comes from working stock – a look at the parents will give you an idea of how the puppy will look when it is adult.

This is not intended to be a gundog training manual, but it is enough to say here that the dog and owner must form a strong relationship. The two commonest mistakes are to advance the training too rapidly and to bore the pupils with endless repetitions of the same, tedious lesson. Training should be play, so that the dog does not realize that it is being taught. The basics, which can be started early, are walking to heel and sitting to command. Once these two are deeply ingrained, you will be well on the road to having a steady dog.

Hunting and retrieving come naturally to true-bred gundogs and puppies will carry old shoes or a rubber ball round in their mouths. The trainer has only to harness and direct this instinct to finding and fetching birds; endless lessons with dummies thrown on an open lawn is the quick way to spoil a dog's natural enthusiasm – he simply grows sick of it. A short, play lesson every day on the morning walk, taking things a step at a time, making it fun and carrying out revision from time to time are the right paths to follow. The appendix at the end of this book includes a list of specialist books which the beginner will find useful. The gundog training books give step-by-step instructions on how to teach your dog proper behaviour and make him an effective shooting aid as well as a good companion.

As a general rule, labradors are often more easy to train than the more highly strung springer; the nervous energy and seemingly inexhaustible zest of the latter can make it hard work for the trainer. There tend to be more badly trained springers in the field than labradors, although a springer is an exciting dog to own. 'Once a springer man, always a springer man' is the old saying. The trainer himself must be patient and not fly into a rage if the pupil does not respond to his teaching: it is easily done, and when you feel yourself becoming cross, it is wise to stop the lesson immediately and take the dog home.

Gradually the dog will learn obedience and control, looking to his handler for instructions, but still with room left for him to use his initiative in the search for a wounded bird. The basic requirements are that, in addition to walking at heel and sitting on command, the dog should be responsive when at a distance, retrieve to hand, hunt as required and not run in to every bird or rampage about. Achieving this standard is not difficult on the training ground, but the transfer from it to the shooting field proper is what many handlers find difficult. The presence of other dogs, the flourishing of guns and the fact that the handler is being distracted by other influences can cause a dog, steady in training, suddenly to go to pieces. To avoid many of the problems, resist the temptation to take the dog to the shooting field until it is at least eighteen months old. Even then it should be a spectator; many a promising dog has been spoiled by being sent after a runner which looked as if it were escaping. 'Months to make: minutes to break' is another old saying which holds much truth. Keep the dog on the lead in the early days and strictly limit his work. He must learn that by no means every bird which falls is his.

Valuable experience may be had in the pigeon or duck hide where the dog is near to the shooter, sitting, watching birds passing, hearing some shooting and yet remaining steady. It is also useful to make the dog accustomed to meeting strangers and other dogs. Take him to the shops, for experience of the hurly-burly and gradually acclimatize the dog to dealing with new situations.

If you decide that, for any reason, you are not yet ready to take on a dog because of anticipated absences from home such as

Perfect delivery by this English springer spaniel.

college, school or a new job, all is not lost. As second best you must cultivate the friendship of someone who does have a dog and whom you may accompany on shooting days; it is not essential for each of you to have a dog, and the same animal can easily do the work for two guns. This is far better than going out on your own with no dog to help you. Also, like many other sports, shooting is very much about making friends and meeting people. Days in the field, even for the wildfowler, are better if there is somebody with whom you may conduct a post-mortem and compare notes afterwards.

An alternative is to borrow a dog. This need not be as absurd as it may sound, and while many dogs may be 'one man dogs', or trained to such an exceptionally high standard as to be not for loan, there are many, perfectly adequate animals which their owners might be prepared to loan to their friends. I once found myself dogless for a year, having unexpectedly lost a faithful labrador in a road accident. A few dogless days in the field quickly reminded me of how joyless and difficult such days can be so I made enquiries and found many kind people who gave me free access to their dogs, but usually with the warning, 'He's not much good, but better than nothing.' They explained any vices the dog might have, and simply invited me to help myself whenever I needed him.

It was an interesting shooting season. Early on a duck-shooting morning I would creep like a burglar, into the friend's back garden, trying desperately to remember the name of the dog I was supposed to be borrowing today. There was also the fervent hope that he would not wake the household with frantic barking as I, the stranger, approached. I must have tried eight or nine dogs at various times that winter: they represented at least three breeds. All did their best, and while, between them, they combined most of the vices known to gundogs, we had a great deal of fun together, not to mention filling the bag on occasions when it would have been a good deal lighter without their help. The experience proved the point that a borrowed dog has its merits, provided its borrower is fully prepared to accept responsibility for its safety and welfare and return it in one piece.

It is now part of the British Association of Shooting and Conservation's (BASC) official policy that wildfowlers and rough shooters should not take the field without a dog. It is a view which I heartily endorse for the reasons I have given. Owning, training and working a gundog add a whole new dimension to the sport of shooting; it is not an opportunity to be lightly passed by.

RULES FOR DOGHANDLING
ON SHOOTING DAYS

Check with your host that your dog is welcome.

Control the dog at all times; do not allow it to fight, disturb livestock or spoil the sport of another gun.

Keep the dog on a lead unless it is rock steady, but always use a lead when walking on the road. Use no dog collar in the field and do not attach the lead to your belt.

See to the comfort of your dog before your own at the end of the day and rub it with a towel or sack if it is wet.

Do not let your dog take a bird from another dog.

Do not allow the dog to retrieve another man's bird.

Do not allow your dog to become overtired or make unreasonable demands upon it.

Do not encourage your dog to cross the boundary onto a neighbour's land, unless you have permission.

11
The Law

I have explained that guns and cartridges are dangerous things and there are strictly enforced laws of the land which exist to ensure the safety of citizens from themselves and from fellow-gun owners. By and large, the laws relating to shooting make good sense and exist for the protection of the general public as well as for the shooters themselves. They aim to deter the unlawful use of guns in criminal offences, prevent dangerous weapons from falling into the wrong hands, such as people under age, and restrict, usually to private ground, the places where guns may legitimately be used. There are countries in the world where few, if any, such laws apply, and the social problems which result would be considered horrendous if they happened in the UK.

The Firearms Act of 1968 defines a shotgun as being a smooth-bore gun with a barrel not less than twenty-four inches in length and not being an air gun. If you wish to possess such a weapon you must acquire a shotgun certificate from the Chief Officer of Police of the area in which you live. There is no age limit for possession of a shotgun certificate but strict rules apply to the age at which young people may buy or own a shotgun.

It is an offence to make a gift of a shotgun and ammunition to a person under the age of fifteen, and no such person may have an assembled shotgun with him unless he is under the direct supervision of a certificate holder aged twenty-one or over, and is acting under that person's instructions, or unless the shotgun is securely fastened in a gun cover in such a way that it cannot be fired.

Someone between fifteen and seventeen years of age may be given or loaned a shotgun or ammunition, but he may not buy them. After reaching the age of fifteen, anyone may use a shotgun without supervision, provided he holds a valid shotgun certificate. Once you are seventeen, you may purchase a shotgun and ammunition but, again, you must have a valid shotgun certificate. There is a slight variation of this which applies if you happen to live in Northern Ireland. The key age below which you may not buy or have in your possession a *firearm* or ammunition is eighteen, but if you are under sixteen this is not an offence provided you are in the company of a certifiate holder aged eighteen plus, if you are on your own land or if you are on land where you live and work.

A shotgun certificate is your right to which you are entitled. Exceptions include those with violent, criminal records or a history of mental instability. The police will issue you with the relevant application form which you must complete, have countersigned in the appropriate place, and return to the police station. Fees tend to increase from time to time, but currently it costs £12.00 to issue a certificate and £8.00 to renew it, but the certificate is valid for three years from the date of issue. Some constabularies may issue you with a reminder that your certificate is about to expire, but the responsibility lies with the owner to see that renewal takes place in proper time. Once your certificate has been allowed to lapse, you are committing an offence if you have a gun in your possession.

When you receive your certificate you must sign it (in ink), and you are obliged to inform the Chief Constable who issued it if any of your shotguns is stolen. If you lose your certificate or have it stolen, technically you are in possession of uncertificated guns and are therefore guilty of an offence. A replacement certificate (currently £8.00) may be obtained but, in any case, the Chief Constable should be informed of your loss. Notify the Chief Constable if you should change your address; failure to do so might result in a delay in renewal when the time comes.

As usual, there are the inevitable exceptions. A shotgun certificate is not required if you are shooting clay pigeons on an official (police-approved) clay pigeon shooting ground or shooting school. Nor do you require one if you are a UK visitor, staying in this country for not more than thirty days in twelve months. You may also, without a certificate, borrow a shotgun from a landowner and use it on his ground in his presence.

A policeman may stop you at any time when you are out shooting and he has the right to see your shotgun certificate. If you fail to produce it, he may confiscate your gun and demand your name and address, so it is wise to have this vital piece of cardboard in a safe, but handy place at all times. Should the police refuse to grant or renew your certificate, you may appeal to the Crown Court within twenty-one days of the refusal. (In Scotland you may appeal to the Sheriff, in Northern Ireland to the Secretary of State.)

It is an offence to have with you, in a public place, a loaded shotgun. A public place includes any highway or any other premises or place to which the public has access, such as parks or playing fields. If you have shooting rights on land through which a footpath or bridleway runs, then you may reasonably carry your loaded gun on or near the footpath. A public place also includes lakes and rivers. You may not shoot within fifty feet of the centre of the highway. It should go without saying that you may not shoot on land where you have no permission to be – unless you have a compelling reason which you may have to justify in court. It is an offence to enter a building while carrying a shotgun unless you have authority.

In 1981 an important piece of legislation called the Wildlife and Countryside Act was passed. This has implications for the sporting shotgunner which he would be wise to learn. It protects all wild birds and their eggs with the exception of birds covered by Game Acts and other designated pests which may be shot at any time. Some birds receive special protection at all times, others in certain seasons, others not at all. Penalties for killing harmless birds or game out of season, are severe.

The following birds may be shot during their open seasons: capercaillie, coot, tufted duck, gadwall, goldeneye, Canada goose, greylag goose, pink-footed goose, white fronted goose (in England and Wales only), mallard, moorhen, pintail, golden plover, pochard, shoveller, common snipe, teal, wigeon, woodcock.

The following 'pest' species may be shot at any time by someone deemed an authorized person, namely the owner or occupier of land where the shooting takes place, or someone with special permission from the County Council: crow, collared dove, greater black-backed gull, lesser black-backed gull, herring gull, jackdaw, jay, magpie, feral pigeon, rook, house sparrow, starling, woodpigeon. The racing pigeon which is likely to fly over you at least once during a day shooting is not listed under any category, but it is a strictly protected bird at all times.

As well as the statutory close seasons on quarry species (see Chapter 8) it is illegal to shoot game birds on a Sunday or on Christmas Day, but there are some counties in England and Wales where Sunday wildfowling is permitted. After a period of prolonged hard weather, the Secretary of State may decide, after consultation with various interested parties, that wildfowl and wader shooting should be temporarily suspended to save the quarry species undue punishment when they are in an emaciated state. Plenty of warning and public notice will be given if and when this takes place.

There are also restrictions on the methods which you may employ to put birds in the bag; the reasons for which should be fairly obvious. You may not use a semi-automatic shotgun which can hold more than three cartridges at once; you may not use lamps to dazzle the quarry; you may not use a live, tethered decoy and you may not pursue birds in any motorized vehicle such as a motor boat or a Landrover. All these provisions aim to prevent what most would hold to be unsporting practices which, if over-employed, would result in over-large bags. The sale of most of the quarry species, with the notable exception of wild geese, is allowed during a period roughly covering its open season but the seller must possess a Game Dealer's licence.

Some mammals, too, are protected; some of which are likely to be encountered at any time when out shooting. They are badger, bats (all species), wild cat, hedgehog, pine marten, otter, polecat and red squirrel. The same limits apply to shooting them as do to shooting birds. The only exceptions are rabbits and hares which may be shot at night, from a vehicle with a light, but only by the landowner or someone especially authorized by him.

As well as a shotgun certificate, a game licence is required to shoot all game species, including woodcock and snipe, but not hares if you are the landowner or his authorized representative. A game licence is available from a post office and costs £6.00 per annum, but licences for shorter periods are available for a lower price.

Finally there is the matter of trespass upon which I have touched

A licence is necessary to shoot and to sell game.

earlier in this chapter. Every inch of land in the UK belongs to someone, and that person either owns the shooting rights or has ceded or rented them to someone else. There are countries where this is not so, but in the British Isles it is a strict rule. Entering private land with your gun but without permission would lay you open to a charge of armed trespass, the penalties for which are severe and may include the permanent confiscation of your gun. Make absolutely sure of your boundaries and be perfectly clear as to what authority you have to be where you are before you start to shoot. Should you be unlucky enough to be brought to court for any shooting offence, it is useless to plead ignorance. The onus is clearly and firmly on you to be an expert in the laws which govern your sport.

I opened this chapter by observing that most of the laws relating to game and shooting were common sense. They are, but the exceptions and minor complications are what tend to confuse. I would guess that very few experienced shooting men can put hand on heart and claim to know the close seasons of every species, the age restrictions on weapon ownership, the clauses and exceptions or be able to quote verbatim the various Game Acts. However, he will make it his business to know those pieces of legislation which apply to his own branch of the sport – he would be foolish indeed to venture out without a good working knowledge of them.

Shooting men who are seen to break the law do themselves and the image of the sport great damage. To claim that, in the half-light, they mistook a barnacle goose for a pink-foot or a grey plover for a golden plover and thus broke the law, is a pathetic argument. Many shooters may have made such errors of identification, but they too have no excuse. If in doubt, hold your fire, is the sound philosophy which will extricate you from a good many potentially difficult shooting situations, both from the point of view of safety and of abiding by the law.

The shooting laws are constantly under review, so it is important to keep abreast of developments and made sure you familiarize yourself with any changes: a subscription to *Shooting Times* will help you to keep up to date.

12

Conduct in the Field

As well as the written rules of shooting, there are a good many which are unwritten and which the sportsman is expected to observe. They have evolved during years of field shooting and usually have a good reason for their existence. I have mentioned some of the rules for handling gundogs in the field, and it is a typical case of common sense dictating current practice. For example, if your dog collects the birds of another gun, to start with that gun cannot try his own dog on them and also there is no record of who has picked up what; time is wasted looking for birds which have already been gathered. If your dog is left wet and muddy while you go in to the fireside the dog will become a victim of rheumatics and other ailments, and in any case that is no way to treat a valued and useful shooting companion who has worked hard for you all day.

Much of what is considered proper etiquette for various shooting occasions will already have appeared in the pages of this book, but a more concentrated catalogue of information will be helpful. Many young and inexperienced shots often find this aspect of the sport the most difficult to assimilate.

On a rough-shooting day you must be sure that you know exactly where you are going and what are the boundaries of the land you have permission to shoot. Be sure that your permission is absolutely certain, and not a vague hint that one day you might be able to come. If in any doubt, telephone the farmer in advance and inform him of your plans – this is good practice in any case. A farmer hearing shots from his field will waste time rushing down to see who is there and you must not put him to this inconvenience. Make sure you are aware of the footpaths and bridle-ways which may pass through the farm; learn the law which applies to shooting on or near them, and remember that members of the public may be walking along them at any time.

Some farmers may give you permission to shoot rabbits and pigeons but not game or wildfowl. The understanding between you should be crystal clear and should be, on your part, strictly observed. The most tempting pheasant must be left alone, if your authority does not extend to game. If you shoot it you will lose your shooting a good deal more easily than you acquired it. If you have authority to shoot game, then you must have a Game Licence, and it is wise to have your shotgun certificate with you at all times.

Match the gun and cartridge to the sort of shooting you are likely to expect. We have seen how the degree of choke and the size of shot will influence range and pattern, and that it is pattern which is all-important. For pigeons you should not be shooting at more than 35 yards with 6 or 7 shot; larger shot and tighter chokes are appropriate to wildfowl, but remember that most shots are taken at well under 35 yards, so open borings and small shot, ie a good pattern at close range, is the ideal for general, all-round shooting (see Chapter 4).

Even a rough-shooting day needs to be properly organized with someone in charge; he must plan the day and make sure that everyone present knows what is going on. He will point out, especially to strangers, where it is unsafe to shoot and places where special care must be taken. He will remind the team of what species may be shot that day. He or any other member of the team has an obligation to condemn dangerous or unsporting shooting. While it is acceptable to fire at 'pest' species while they are at very close range, poor fliers or even sitters, it is not acceptable to shoot thus at game or wildfowl. A pheasant blasted down at ten-yards range is an unsporting shot and is useless to eat. Do not allow such events to pass without comment. However, shooting at excessive ranges, even at 'pest' species is never acceptable and is, if anything, worse than close-range blasting; it can lead only to wounding and lost birds and again, such conduct should be openly condemned at all times. An easy bird for you might provide a better shot for a companion, so do not earn the reputation of a greedy or too keen a shot. Leave such a bird for a neighbour and people will not fail to notice.

'Keeping a good line' is important. If one gun hurries forward or lags behind, he is vulnerable to shots from those at each side of him whose angle of fire he has limited. The rule is to take the pace of the slowest; guns of widely differing ages over varied terrain will have very varied paces, so stick to the speed of the slowest and do not hesitate to call for a halt if you are tired or have an obstacle to cross; moreover, point out to neighbours if you feel they are hurrying ahead. A slow pace will show you more game and better sport than will a mad gallop.

When shooting over farmland, have a respect for hedges, gates, trees, crops and livestock. Do not damage or interfere with any of them. The farmer will notice, and remember that he is your strongest ally. In the same way, do not overshoot. To kill more than you can carry or need is greedy and endangers stock for next year and the year after. Remember that you are shooting with the future in mind. The exception to this principle might be pigeon or rabbit shooting to protect crops where no limits apply. However, to set yourself a bag limit of game per day or per season, a figure based on the success of the breeding year and your efforts as an amateur keeper, is no bad policy.

Problems occur near boundaries: you should know well enough where they lie, but it is inevitable that, sooner or later, a bird shot on your side will fall or run onto a neighbour's ground. It is best to anticipate this and make a reciprocal arrangement with him to pick such birds on each other's ground. If you have done so and you do cross over to make a retrieve, it is wise to leave your gun on your own side of the fence. Relationships with his neighbours are, to a shooting man, matters of great importance.

Finally, at the end of the day, make sure that you take home your litter with you. Lunch bags and beer tins are obvious, but many shooters are more casual with their cartridge cases which are mostly made of plastic and do not rot down as paper ones would. Orange, red and green plastic cylinders accumulated over a season, make the countryside look unsightly. It is an easy enough matter to keep spent cases in your bag or pocket and dispose of them when you arrive home.

When you do reach home, all is not over for there is a strict order of events which the shooting man ought to follow. He must first see to his dog, clean it, check its feet for cuts, make sure it is dry, feed it and see it safely and comfortably bedded down for the night. Next, the gun must be given a good cleaning and put away in your secure place. Follow the instructions given in Chapter 3. Thirdly, take any game which may have been your share of the bag and hang it in a cool place, out of reach of cats and rats and out of direct sunlight. In warm weather blow-flies can be a problem, but fly-proof larders of the sort used by caravanners are the answer, unless you have one of the old-fashioned meat safes. Care for and respect for the quarry, even after it is dead, is an important ethic of shooting.

The formal driven shoot, to which reference has been made throughout this book, was perfected in the UK during the Edwardian era, when the gentlemen sportsmen of the day made huge bags of pheasants, grouse and partridges. Our quiet discipline and tight organization of a well-planned driven day remain the envy of the shooting world. On most estates the numbers of the slain will be less than in the bad, old days, but the principles of a keeper and a team of beaters driving the ground in a carefully thought out way

A dog must be cared for if it is to give good service.

towards guns strategically placed so that good, sporting birds are shown are as sound as ever. The organization of such a day is complex and wide-ranging and must take into account transport of guns and beaters, lunch arrangements, planning drives, liaison with farm staff, payment of helpers and a multitude of other things, not least of which is the natural anxiety of a host about the weather, the conduct of the birds and whether his guests are having an enjoyable day.

The host will, like the rough shooter, have his eye on the future, and will organize things so that testing birds are shown and not just easy ones which will not challenge the guns and too many of which they will be likely to shoot. He will be seen to care for his game in other ways such as by appointing a proper team of pickers-up to find lost birds, and will have set aside space in a vehicle for the carrying of game and a cool safe place where it may be stored and exhibited with pride. No good host allows shot game to be trampled underfoot in the muddy well of a Landrover where it will quickly become spoiled. The organizer will also arrange for a dry luncheon shed to be available: there will be no doubt in anyone's mind that he is in charge of the occasion.

To be invited on such a shoot as a guest is to receive a generous gift. The provision of driven shooting is the most expensive side of shooting, even on an un-keepered farm. A reared pheasant cannot be produced for much under £10.00, so to shoot a hundred means that someone has paid out roughly £1000. Whether you go as a guest or whether you have paid money to buy a driven day, it must be regarded as an important ocasion when the conventions must be observed – conventions which some would regard as quite as important as your marksmanship.

Arrive on time having replied promptly to the invitation and wear clean and suitable clothing (see Chapter 6). Find out if lunch is provided or whether you are expected to bring your own. Establish whether or not your dog will be welcome, but if in doubt or if you are at all unsure of his steadiness, leave him at home. There will be other dogs there to pick up birds, and you will have one thing less to worry about and be able to concentrate on your shooting. When the draw for position is made, remember your number and what the arrangement is for advancing between drives. Different shoots have different conventions, and it is surprising how many quite old hands forget their numbers – especially after lunch!

Your adherence to the safety rules, it goes without saying, will be impeccable, and you will take no risky shots, shoot down the line or allow your gun to point at a fellow-shooter or beater. Carry the gun in the slip between drives for the reasons explained in Chapter 5: this will protect it and also ensure that it cannot be accidentally discharged. When you arrive at your stand you will already have found out if the host wishes some species not to be shot; some hosts will have decreed a 'cocks only' day or decided, because of their dwindling numbers, not to shoot any hares. At the peg, make sure you are fully aware of where everyone is standing, especially your immediate neighbouring guns, stops and pickers-up. Acknowledge that you have seen each other by raising your hat or your hand, but on no account ever shout or call out in the shooting field. Game is not deaf, and a whole drive may be ruined by one thoughtless gun bellowing at his dog. Make sure you know from which direction to expect the beaters and glance round to check that there is no farm work taking place. In addition remind yourself of the distance and angle of any buildings. It is important to stay at the peg or in the position where your host has placed you. Do not wander around or reposition yourself for any reason even if it may, at the time, seem good to you. Remain silent at all times at the peg and do not cry out cheerful greetings to fellow-guns or shout to warn them of approaching birds.

As on the rough shoot, make sure that you have a Game Licence and that your shotgun certificate is to hand. A useful extra which, in my opinion, every shooter ought to have, is insurance cover for third-party liability. In spite of the care you take, an accident might, one day happen, and litigation is an expensive business. You will be expected to come to the shoot unaccompanied, and if you wish to bring wife, husband or girl-friend, then you must, in advance, confirm that this is acceptable. Make sure that he or she is suitably dressed in neutral colours for, as well as not being deaf, game is certainly not blind. Mark down any birds you have hit but which have travelled on or dropped afar. Tell the picker-up or your host precisely where you think it went down, and if and when the picker-up recovers it, be sure to thank him.

There will be clear signals to indicate the start and end of drives. Never shoot except between these signals. As you walk away from the end of a drive, a most tempting bird may rise from your very feet, but resist the natural urge to fire. The great occasion, the flowing of adrenalin and your feelings of excitement can make you do dangerous things or act out of character: remain calm and keep a clear head and cool judgement. As on the rough shoot, do not be greedy and shoot birds travelling towards another gun. Leave a bird which may be over you but which will give him a better shot – people will notice such things. A doubtful bird which flies between you is better left than shared. It is acceptable to break the no-talking rule and call 'Yours' and leave it for him – again you collect a good mark.

On no account claim a doubtful bird as yours if both of you should happen to fire. Always give the other chap the credit. Keep your opinions to yourself unless asked and do not boast about mighty feats in the shooting field or amazingly difficult birds you have killed. It is perfectly natural for you to wish to create a good impression, but this is done far more effectively by your calmness, modesty, safety and general demeanour. No one is impressed by boasting which often has the opposite effect. It does not do to claim everything which flies near you. The really great shots would allow easy birds to pass them by unshot at, or left for neighbours, while they would pick what they felt were the really difficult ones. It is not done to appear over-keen.

By the same token, long shots should be avoided for they result in wounded or lost birds. At the end of the day thank the keeper, head beater and pickers-up who will have worked hard to provide your sport. On keepered shoots it is customary to tip the keeper. There is no standard sum and, clearly, some people can afford to tip more generously than others. A rule of thumb is £10.00 per hundred birds shot, but a boy with only his pocket money on which to rely would not care to go so high. If you are asked to a shoot, ask your father or a knowledgeable friend for advice. The keeper will almost invariably hand you a brace of birds at the end of the day, and that is your opportunity to thank him and discreetly hand him his tip. Make sure you leave no litter behind you; you will have picked up your cartridge cases of course, but is is inconvenient for someone to have to post on to you the waterproof trousers or hat which you have forgotten.

On arrival home go into your standard routine of seeing to dog, gun, game and self, in that order, and do not forget to record your adventures in your shooting diary while they are still fresh in your mind. The following day, write a brief letter of thanks to your host; this little courtesy costs nothing but a little time and a stamp, and is much appreciated.

The third main area of shooting which has its special code is wildfowling. We have looked at some of the techniques involved but there is a code of practice which ought to be followed. Nothing could be further removed from the strict formality of the covert shoot, for the fowler is usually on his own or with one companion so there is no one to censure his actions.

It is vital that he understands the boundaries of where he intends to shoot. Most foreshores are the property of either the Crown Commissioners or a private landowner whose land runs down to the coast. Much of this land in England and Wales is now administered by BASC-affiliated, local wildfowling clubs and you must be a member to shoot or have bought a day or week ticket, a limited number of which are sometimes available. In Scotland, the

Never send your dog for another man's bird.

Crown retains rights on the foreshore and they are available to the general public unless a special country park or nature reserve has been created over the area.

Saltmarshes can be dangerous places with soft mud and quicksands to trap the unwary. Sudden fogs may roll in from the sea. You may be high and dry on a little eminence well out in the marsh, but the tide may creep round behind you, between yourself and safety, and cut you off. Any one of these events could prove fatal and each year there are accidents and tragedies. Learn the marsh, do not go unaccompanied onto dangerous ground. A large-scale map is useful and you should plan your expedition with care, well in advance. Tell someone where you are going and give a rough indication of what time you can be expected back. Let them know when you have returned safely, a precaution all too often overlooked.

Buy a copy of the tide-table and study it. Beware of going onto the marsh if a very high tide is expected, but knowing the time of high water will enable you to make your way off before the water catches you up or cuts you off. It goes without saying that a watch, preferably waterproof, should be part of the fowler's essentials. A compass is vital because the most experienced hand can be lost in a fog in no time, but if you have taken a bearing for a safe return route, you will never be lost. A barrel blocked with snow or mud can, as we have seen, burst a gun and injure the shooter; blockages are more likely on the marsh than anywhere, so carry a pull-through in your bag. A weight, a cord and a loop of rag are all you need, but it might be enough to save your day's sport. Make it a habit to glance down your barrels before you load and between shots.

A torch is sometimes recommended, though it is not in my view essential but sometimes useful. Night vision and dilated pupils are good enough. A flashing torch disturbs fowl, leaves you as blind as a bat when you switch it off and is extra weight. However, it can save your life in an emergency by attracting rescuers to your position. More handy is a stout wading pole with which you can pick out soft places and feel your way across flooding creeks. Binoculars are a useful accessory, but they should be lightweight.

If you intend to be out for a long period, take a supply of food and a hot drink in a flask. Alcohol is not a good accompaniment to any sort of shooting, and the semblance of warmth which a swig from a flask can give is purely illusory. In reality it has the opposite to the desired effect. A good, big bag is very useful, for it can double as a waterproof seat.

Clothing should be warm, rugged, waterproof and of a colour

which blends well with the background. Thigh-length waders are better than short wellingtons for you will often be kneeling down or floundering in water more than knee deep. A fowler often seeks his sport in the worst weather and he is miserable and shoots badly if he is inadequately clothed.

Wildfowling may be carried out in lonely, remote place, but it is surprising how many people know what you are doing. Birdwatchers with telescopes and other fowlers will look in your direction when they hear a shot, and it is important that you do the right thing. You are as much an ambassador for your sport on the saltmarsh as you are on the most important covert shoot which ever existed.

Your quarry is an internationally shared resource; numbers cannot be replenished by artificial rearing, and while it is quite proper to shoot, conservation must be in your mind, especially when the birds are easy and a large bag possible. Long-range shooting is, if anything, more reprehensible in wildfowling than in any other branch of the sport. Wildfowl can carry shot and travel great distances when wounded and in the half-light or over hostile terrain it is virtually impossible to retrieve such birds. Dead or dying birds found on roadsides by farmers, birdwatchers and members of the public do the image of the sport little good. Just one foolish or irresponsible act brings the whole body of shooting men into disrepute.

Have regard for other fowlers. Do not bang your car door, play a radio, shout or in any other way disturb their shooting. If you arrive late for flight in the morning and walk across the marsh, or if you hide too near another gun, you will have a detrimental effect on everyone's sport. You are all on the same side, and you can imagine how you would feel if a late arrival settled in between your position and the line you expected the fowl to follow. Pick up your litter and spent cartridge cases and demolish unsightly hides or holes in the mud before leaving.

In other sorts of shooting a dog is recommended; in lone fowling it is essential. A bird has only to fall across a flooded creek or begin to drift out to sea and it is lost. A wounded bird will run or swim away at some speed. A fowler's dog should be hardy, good in water, patient and prepared to 'rough it' with you in a muddy creek. Do what you can to make its life a little more easy by sitting it in a dry place and out of the worst of the weather. On arrival home be especially careful to see that the dog is cleaned, dried, fed and bedded down. Many fowlers' dogs are plagued by rheumatism in later life: it can be attributed directly to frequent wettings. As usual, no matter how tired or hungry you may be pay special attention to cleaning the gun, for salt water, sea air, mud and sand are death to it. Hang up your birds properly in a cool, dry place. See that none of them is wasted, for to shoot a bird you are not prepared to eat, unless it is a pest species, undermines one of the underlying philosophies of shooting. If you cannot eat it or give it to someone who you know will, do not shoot it.

In all sorts of shooting, it is inevitable that wounded birds will occasionally come to hand. These must be instantly dispatched by the shooter by giving them a sharp blow where the head joins the neck with a heavy blunt instrument such as a stout stick. On no account use your gun as a club – it has been known to happen. Some shooters carry with them a short weighted club made of wood or staghorn, similar to that used by fishermen to dispatch fish. This is called a priest (because it administers the last rites) and is recommended for anyone who has the slightest anxiety about their ability to kill game. 'Pulling the neck' of a bird is learned only after much practice, and the twirling round of a bird by the head which we see so often these days, is next to useless.

This may appear a formidable list of things to master but a keen beginner tends to be a receptive pupil: he has the greatest incentive of all to do well. Most of the other people in the shooting field will be kind and helpful and will be delighted to answer any questions you may ask. Be philosophical if you shoot badly or well and do not point out either fact to your fellow-shooters. Robert Churchill once remarked, 'Do not tell the other guns you are shooting badly: they will have noticed!' Keep quiet about your own showing, but praise good shooting and congratulate the poor shot on any good shot he has achieved; this is most heartening for him, and someone may do the same for you one day.

Above all, remember you are there to have fun, so enjoy it!

13

Various

The British Association for Shooting and Conservation (the BASC) has cropped up several times in these pages. It is the main national organization for the shooting man, it fights for his cause in the national and international arenas, provides a good, personal insurance policy, issues a colourful quarterly magazine, manages some foreshore shooting through the affiliated clubs, initiates research programmes, runs an education policy, shotgun coaching and is very much in evidence at many country shows and fairs throughout the summer. Every shotgun owner ought to be a member, but sadly there are too many who seem prepared, selfishly, not to belong, but to continue their sport while others fight their battles for them. Every shooter not a member undermines the BASC's strength and diminishes the power of its lobby. There are almost a million shotgun owners, and their combined voice would carry considerable weight when restrictions on their sport are threatened.

The British Field Sports Society (BFSS) is another important national body whose brief includes not only shooting but also fishing and hound sports. The concept that all field sports should stand together is a sound one, for some of our opponents make no secret of the fact that they will not be happy until all of them are banned. The BFSS has a powerful voice in the corridors of power and some influence behind the parliamentary scene. Many shooting men are members both of the BASC and the BFSS.

The Clay Pigeon Shooting Association (CPSA) is what its name implies, the national body for the clay bird person. It too provides insurance for its members, access to some clay grounds, courses for coaches and shots. Most formal clay shoots and clubs are run under CPSA rules, and most clay shooters become members of the CPSA, for it makes good sense for them to do so.

The British Deer Society (BDS) is for deer men and thus of no interest to the shotgunner, for all deer, to all intents and purposes, must now be shot only with a high-powered rifle. Other specialist bodies exist, notably the Game Conservancy, an independently financed body which carries out research into the shooting man's practical problems. These include dealing with changing conditions and helping game and wildlife to adapt to increasing farming pressures which restrict game numbers. It helps landowners, farmers and rough shooters to make the most of their shooting assets and ensures that the Government and ministries are constantly made aware that game is important as are its necessary conservation and management, which in turn benefit other forms of wildlife. There are now in hand fourteen research projects covering different aspects of gamebird, wildfowl, and deer biology and management, some of them financed by special grants or groups of sponsors.

A network of skilled game advisers is available for on-the-shoot consultations, for improving habitat, showing birds to the best advantage, or improving breeding success on the rearing field and in the wild. Reducing shoot costs is an important aspect of this work. Annual residential courses for gamekeepers are held at Fordingbridge (Hampshire) as well as courses for young shots and part-time gamekeepers. Symposia are held from time to time on specialized subjects. In addition, courses are held at various centres up and down the country on all aspects of game and deer management. A three-day stalkers' course in Scotland is a regular feature. Staff are available to give lectures on a variety of topics to farmers' clubs and the like or through sponsorship at open meetings.

Descriptions of research work in progress appear in the *Annual Review*, published each May. Also, regular newsletters keep members fully in touch, and announcements of current interest are published through general release to the Press. Most regions in the country have their own branch which arranges interesting outings and functions and often an annual dinner for members and guests.

Other associations which may be of interest to the shooting man will include the Kennel Club, the national body which promotes the general improvement of standards for dogs, dog shows, field trials, working tests and obedience classes. The Kennel Club is responsible for licensing shows, framing and enforcing the rules governing exhibition of dogs and conduct of field trials: it also keeps a record of shows, trials and obedience tests. The Muzzle Loaders Association of Great Britain encourages the collection and restoration of old weapons and also their use at targets, clays and game. The National Air Rifle and Pistol Association promotes the use of air weapons. The Guild of Taxidermists, the Game Farmers Association, the National Game Dealers Association and the Gun Trade Association are mostly professional bodies, but they all play their part in furthering the sport of shooting and protecting the interests of shooters.

An important organization which represents all our field sports in the wider arena of the EEC is the Fédération des Associations des Chasseurs Européens (FACE) through which the UK is able to monitor all comment and proposed legislation affecting in any way the conduct of our sports. FACE (UK) is financed by donations from members of the public and from its constituent organizations. These include the British Deer Society, the British Falconers Club, the British Field Sports Society, the Game Conservancy, the British Association for Shooting and Conservation and the Salmon and Trout Association.

There is a specialist club or association for every shooting man and the three major bodies, to at least one of which he ought to belong, the BASC, the BFSS and the Game Conservancy. For the cost of about 100 cartridges to join, the shooter receives good value for money and may properly feel that he is making a contribution to the future of his sport.

Shotgun shooting is a broad-based sport with a sub-culture, language, lore, tradition and codes of practice all its own. This book has given an indication of the many aspects, each a miniature field of specialization, which go to make it up and of which the layman knows little. The shooter likes to surround himself with the trappings and reminders of his sport. We have seen how keenly he may collect badges and pin-feathers for his hat or how he likes to surround himself with various accessories, many of which, to be frank, are of little practical use to him. The more aesthetic side of shooting may be partly satisfied by books and pictures which many sportsmen like to collect.

Sad to say, such things tend to be expensive, but collecting does appeal to the hoarding instant in one's nature and, even today, bargains may be found. Old shooting books bought from an antiquarian bookseller, have become collectors' items and what once could be bought for a few pence, now cost many pounds. Wildfowling books by the old masters of the Victorian age are probably top of the price league. Writers such as Peter Hawker, Sir Ralph Payne Gallwey, Millais, St John and others of that larger than life, extrovert stamp are now hard to find. However, some of them have been reproduced as facsimile reprints, or edited and reprinted in later, cheap editions and are correspondingly less expensive to buy. Within the last thirty or forty years there has been a plethora of books on wildlife, sport and the countryside, most of which have run to only one edition because of the limitations of the market. These are much less expensive than the leather-bound sagas of the foreshore, and they represent a fascinating way of learning the background to sport as it is today, how things have changed and developed, and much of interest about birds and beasts.

Books by 'BB', Williamson, Peter Scott, Richard Jefferies, Bill Powell and many others who wrote of sport and country matters forty years ago are easy enough to buy and make excellent reading for their own sakes. From a collector's point of view, you have to start somewhere, and the oldest rule of that game is that what is cheap today is likely to be more valuable tomorrow. No one is printing any more of these older books, so the supply will always be limited. Hunt the second-hand bookshops, junk shops, Scouts' jumble sales, and now and again you will find something of interest. I once came across a copy of Jefferies' *The Amateur Poacher* and *The Gamekeeper at Home*, two volumes in one, on a stall at the church fête. It cost three (old) pence and has been a treasured possession ever since. When not actually engaged in shooting, there are few things a shooter likes doing more than talking or reading about his sport. New shooting books appear regularly in the bookshops, and every shooting man should have a carefully made selection of them within arm's length of his fireside chair.

There is other reading matter which you should consider such as magazines which cater for the shooting man, and while they too are not cheap, it is important that you subscribe to at least one of them. We live in changing times with new developments rushing in at every turn. The protection of the curlew and its removal from the list of quarry species, restrictions on snares, new regulations pertaining to semi-automatic shotguns, the sudden imposition of a hard-weather shooting ban – all have happened in recent memory. How is the shooter to know about them if not through his papers and periodicals? Being well informed is, perhaps, more important in shooting than in many other activities.

There are specialist magazines such as *Guns Review*, but for a wider, all-round view, I mention three. One is the house magazine of Gilbertson and Page, the old firm of dog food and keepering equipment, and called *Dog and Country*. This gives a good, balanced view of the country scene with fair coverage of all field sports. Also monthly is *Sporting Gun* from East Midlands Allied Press which covers only shotgun shooting, with plenty for the clayshooter, reviews of weapons and a fixture list of clay pigeon shoots. The best-known and oldest shooting magazine is *Shooting Times*, published weekly, a good blend of entertainment, informa-

Many shooting men are amateur taxidermists.

tion and advertisement which constantly emphasizes the inter-relationship of all field sports and their dependence, one upon the other. There is an understandable bias in favour of all shooting matters.

Other minor spin-offs include taxidermy, an art in its own right and popular with some shooting folk. It was fashionable in Victorian times, fell into disfavour and now is making a strong come-back. Shooters sometimes like to preserve a special bird they have shot, such as a first woodcock, a blackcock with its striking, curly tail or the heads of geese. It is fairly easy to attain to a reasonable level of proficiency in this art.

It all goes to prove that there is much more to shooting than just pulling the trigger of a gun.

14
The Shooting Ethic

Ever since mankind lived in caves he has hunted animals, wildfowl and edible birds, first for food and secondly as a means of recreation. As time passed and greater degrees of civilization were reached, the need to hunt for food diminished whereas the desire to hunt did not. Thus, hunting became a sport and with it arrived the ethics, codes of behaviour and traditions which these pages have explained. An integral part of shooting is a respect for the quarry and the countryside, and a consideration for all other users of and dwellers in the countryside.

The shooter must be aware of other pressures on the countryside, pressures of forestry, high-intensity farming, land draining and pollution, but what has to be realized is that increased leisure time and mobility have rendered the countryside more accessible to more people than ever before. It all means that the shooter must be aware of legal restrictions and self-imposed codes of practice in the conduct of his sport. This knowledge comes with experience, from talking to and asking questions of other sportsmen and reading the right books. Going shooting without the right body of knowledge is as foolish and prodigal as taking an air rifle to shoot geese, and puts you at risk of endangering yourself, your fellow-man and the environment, not to mention bringing your chosen sport and other sportsmen into disrepute.

The word 'conservation' has been mentioned often in this book, and this is the aspect of shooting which the general public finds it hard to comprehend. How is it possible to kill and also conserve? Shooting is a part of the overall plan of management of natural resources which can no longer manage on their own without Man to cull overpopulations, improve the habitat, control predators and take an interest. Each year 30,000 acres of countryside are destroyed by urban development, hedges are being ripped out to enlarge fields, and woodlands felled.

The shooting man will do what he can to promote the breeding of populations of his quarry species, and by doing so, save the

woodlands, small mammals, song birds, wild flowers and butterflies which share the same environment. He and the farmer have a
vital role to play in ensuring that there will be a countryside and
fauna and flora to show to the generations who are still to come.
He has the countryside in trust, and his grandchildren will judge
him by his actions when the time comes. It is a fact that the
birdwatcher, pure conservationist and those who make the most
fuss about our dwindling countryside, and who are often those
antagonistic to field sports, make little practical contribution to
their heritage. The man struggling down a muddy ride with a sack
of corn on his back, setting traps for the rats, waiting patiently for
the thieving crow, paying out his hard-earned money to buy
pheasant chicks, planting trees in spring whose foot is most often
on the ground he manages is likely to be a shooting man and not
one who simply pays lip-service to conservation. Many may be
found to speak passionately about it as an abstract concept, but all
too few will actually take off their coats and get down to work.

The result of good practice and a careful custodianship of our
sport is that Britain, despite its geographical restrictions and
over-large population has some of the best and most sought-after
shooting in the world. The development of the sporting shotgun
from flintlock to breech-loader matched the changing patterns of
agriculture, while the private ownership of land has ensured a
flourishing population of game. Despite the pressures on the
countryside our game and wildfowl numbers are as flourishing as
at any time.

It is no longer possible for the beginner to pick up a gun and
walk into the nearest field or even down to the foreshore and start
to shoot. It is because he cannot act thus that we have such a
healthy population of quarry species. However, there are, as we
have seen, many routes into the sport, via beating, pigeon
shooting, finding a little place you can share with a few friends,
buying some shooting, cultivating a farming friend or any of the
other ways I have indicated. Clay pigeon shooting is nationally
established and popular, and most clubs will welcome new members. The dog world is always ready for recruits and there is no
reason why a beginner who has any initiative or 'get up and go'
should not find himself a patch in the sport which, once it is
cultivated and developed will be a growing and increasingly
rewarding territory.

Every aspect of the sport is backed up by a vast body of
expertise and a thriving market place of suppliers of every
conceivable accessory from dog leads to pheasant food, from
shooting vehicles to re-loading tools. You have chosen to follow an

excellent, challenging and rewarding sport. The more expert and knowledgeable you become, the more you will derive from it. Enjoy it, make the most of it and pass it on to the next generation enhanced and better than you found it. Always have in your mind those famous words of HM King George VI which have become the motto of *Shooting Times*:

'The wildlife of today is not ours to dispose of as we please. We must account for it to those who come after.

The shooting man is a custodian of the British countryside.

Appendix 1

Some useful books

'BB', *Tide's Ending*. Tideline
'BB', *Dark Estuary*. Tideline
Beacon Publishing, *The Shooting Handbook* (Annual)
Charlton, Jack, and Tony Jackson, *Field Sports*. Stanley and
  Paul
Coats, Archie, *Pigeon Shooting*. Deutsch
          The Amateur Keeper
Cradock, C., *A Manual of Clay Shooting*. Batsford
Game Conservancy, *The Complete Book of Game Conserva-
tion*. Barrie and Jenkins
Humphreys, John, *The Do-It-Yourself Gameshoot*. David
          and Charles
          Modern Pigeon Shooting. Tideline
Irving, J., *Training Spaniels*. David and Charles
McDougall, Douglas, *Goose Fever*. Published by the author
Moxon, P.R.A., *Gundogs, Training and Field Trials*. Popu-
lar Dogs
Martin, Brian, *Sporting Birds of the British Isles*. David and
Charles
Turner, G. (and others), *Handbook of Shooting (The Sport-
ing Shotgun)*. Pelham Books
Willock, C., *The ABC of Shooting*. Deutsch
          Duck Shooting
Wood, *Taxidermy for You*. Tideline

Appendix 2

Some useful addresses

Arms and Armour Society
40 Great James Street
Holborn WC1

Birmingham Gun Barrel Proof House
Banbury Street
Birmingham 5

British Association for Shooting
and Conservation
Marford Mill
Rossett
Wrexham
Clwyd LL12 0HL

British Deer Society
The Mill House
Bishopstrow
Warminster
Wiltshire

British Falconers Club
P.T. Fields
3 Orchard Lane
Longton
Preston PR4 5AY

British Field Sports Society
59 Kennington Road
London SE1 7PZ

British Field Sports Society (Scotland)
Glenmore Lodge
Moffat
Dumfriesshire

British Pistol Club
251 Hurst Road
Sidcup
Kent

British Sporting Rifle Club
7 Grove Gardens
Frimley
Camberley
Surrey

British Trust for Ornithology
Beech Grove
Tring
Hertfordshire

British Waterfowl Association
Market Place
Haltwhistle
Northumberland

Clay Pigeon Shooting Association
107 Epping New Road
Buckhurst Hill
Essex IG9 5TQ

Council for the Protection of Rural
    England
Hobart Place
London SW1

Country Landowners' Association
16 Belgrave Square
London SW1

Falconry Centre
Newent
Gloucestershire GL18 1JF

Fell and Moorland Working Terrier Club
J. Winch
6 Ascot Road
Shotley Bridge
Co. Durham

Forestry Commission
231 Corstorphine Road
Edinburgh EH12 7AT

Game Conservancy
Burgate Manor
Fordingbridge
Hampshire

Game Farmers' Association
S. Jervis-Read
Walnut Tree Farm
Charing
Ashford
Kent

Gun Trade Association
K. Topping
22 Park Gate Road
Cannock Wood
Rugeley
Staffordshire WS15 4RN

Irish Clay Pigeon Shooting Association
20 Butterfield Drive
Rathfarnham
Dublin 14
Eire

(Irish) Field and Country Sports Society
M.C.A. Jackson
Cooleven
Manor Avenue
Greystones
Co. Wicklow
Eire

Kennel Club
1 Clarges Street
London W1

London Proof House
The Gunmakers Company
48 Commercial Road
London E1

Muzzle Loaders Association of Great Britain
Hon. Sec.
30 Park Road
Hampton Wick
Kingston-upon-Thames
Surrey

National Coursing Club
35–7 Grosvenor Gardens
London SW1W 0BS

National Rifle Association
Bisley Camp
Brookwood
Woking
Surrey

Nature Conservancy
19–20 Belgrave Square
London SW1X 8PY

Red Deer Commission
J. Dooner
82 Fairfield Road
Inverness

Royal Society for the Protection of Birds
The Lodge
Sandy
Bedfordshire

Scottish Clay Pigeon Association
42 Hill Street
Tillicoultry
Clackmannanshire

Scottish Shooting Council
1 Saxe Coburg Place
Edinburgh

Shooting Sports Trust Limited
22 Park Gate Road
Cannock Wood
Rugeley
Staffordshire WS15 4RN

Ulster Clay Pigeon Shooting Association
6 Springhill Avenue
Bangor
Co Down
Northern Ireland

Welsh Clay Pigeon Shooting Association
Trefrane
Roch
Haverfordwest
Dyfed

Wildfowl Trust
Slimbridge
Gloucestershire

World Pheasant Association
Daw's Hall
Lamarsh
Bures
Suffolk CO8 5EX

Index

safety 14, 15; and airguns 21; and
children 78; in clay shooting 83,
84-5; equipment for 54; in the
field 73-9, 103-4, 121, 123, 148,
149, 152-3; and gassing fox
earths 130; law and 35, 143; in
gun handling 36, 76, 123; and
gun storage 41, 54-5; in rabbit
shooting 18, 76-7, 121, 123; and
wildfowling 105-6, 156
safety catch 36, 74
shooting butts 77
Shooting Developments Ltd. 53,
70, 110
shooting diary 60-2, 104, 154
shooting down the line 77
shooting schools 85
shooting seasons 124
shooting sticks 56
Shooting Times 11, 16, 104, 111,
139, 147, 162-3
shot 44; buying 48; for crows 128;
dangers of 76-7; for geese 111;
loading 48-9; and pattern see
pattern, size of 44, 50, 149
shot stringing 28
shotgun certificate 143-4, 149, 153
sidelock action 36
snares 130, 133, 162
snipe 15, 44, 104, 124, 145
Sporting Gun 162
syndicates 49, 134

taxidermy 163
teal 15, 107, 124, 145
Thorpe, MacKenzie 59, 110-11
thumbstick 55-6
traps 129, 130, 131; for clays 85-6
trespass 146-7
triggers 36; gripping 79

vermin 118-19, 123; control of 19,
123, 125, 127-32, 134; ground
128-9; shootable 145, 149;
winged 127-8; and see predators

walking-up 18, 95-6, 98, 99, 104;
guns for 31, 32
Walsingham, Lord 95
waxproof garments 68-9
wigeon 106-7, 114, 124, 145; call
for 59
Wildfowl Trust 111, 172
Wildfowlers Association of Great
Britain and Ireland (WAGBI)
119, 126
wildfowling 16-17, 24, 105-6, 108,
112; abuse of 125; books on 161;
boots for 70, 157; and calls 59;
choke for 50; clothing for 64,
65-6, 156-7; clubs for 16, 17;
code of 154-8; and conservation
145, 157; dangers of 105-6, 156;
decoys for 58-9, 106; and dogs
146, 157-8; equipment for 53, 54,
106, 156; guns for 31-2, 37, 38,
44-5; hides for 56-7; range for 50,
149, 157; seasons for 124, 145;
shot for 44, 149; Sunday 145; and
wounded birds 157, 158; and see
ducks, geese, mallard
wildlife 19, 91-3, 131-2, 164-5 and
see conservation, vermin
Wildlife and Countryside Act
(1981) 130, 145
woodcock 103-4; pin-feathers of
61, 72, 104; season for 124, 145;
shooting 15, 103-4, (and safety)
76, 97, 103-4; shot for 44
woodpigeon see pigeon
wounded game 26, 44, 111, 123,
135-6, 140, 154, 157, 158 and see
runners